UNLOCKING THE SECRETS TO SUCCESSFUL PARENTING

AN EASY-TO-FOLLOW GUIDE FOR RAISING CONFIDENT, HAPPY, AND SUCCESSFUL KIDS

JAMES DUDELSON

CONTENTS

ACKNOWLEDGMENTS

My deepest gratitude to my producer Ana Clavell, whose constant research, prodding, and deadline-setting kept me on track, inspired, and focused.

To my children and grandchildren.

PREFACE

My experience of parenting spans seven decades: I grew up in the '50s, came of age in the '60s, married in the '70s, had my first two children in the '80s, raised them into the late '90s - when they left for college, married and started families of their own - and into the 21st century, with the birth of my youngest, Aaron, who is now 8-years-old.

Looking back, the '50s were a kind of a Parenting Paradox - it was both a stricter time yet, on the other hand, a more liberal time for kids.

I played outside without a parent watching my every move. I walked to school by myself, which I started to do at age 5 when we lived in Iowa.

Besides learning the basic rules of "Never talk to strangers" and "Never take candy from a stranger even if it's candy you love," I never felt threatened by the world out there.

What really scared me was the "wait until your Dad gets home" I got from Mom when I misbehaved. Boy, would that put the fear of God in me! I knew it would be a bad evening.

I would fearfully wait for when my father got home. Then, as soon as he had a moment to take off his hat and put down his briefcase, my Mom would take him into their bedroom to discuss with him what Jimmy had done wrong.

I would try to listen outside their door. Then, when my parents were done talking, I would make a beeline for my room. I felt like a prisoner awaiting sentencing.

My father would come in with a stern look on his face and slowly start taking off his belt.

I envied kids whose fathers wore suspenders.

Seeing him with the belt in his hand was scary enough. That action by itself was more upsetting and painful than the spankings I would get, and I did get plenty! Because, if we're going to call a spade a spade, I was a little terror.

And yet, I recall saying to myself "I will never spank my kids when I grow up."

When I became a parent myself, I recognized that I suffered from a short fuse, just like my Dad. Yet, as tempted as I was a couple of times, I never spanked my kids. I once did a soft slap on my daughter when she was young on her rear end, when she was young. Although I know it didn't hurt her, she cried, and I immediately understood why: just like when my Dad would have his belt in his hand, my daughter was upset by seeing my hand raised. I felt so terrible. It reminded me that I had made a commitment when I was a kid myself.

On that day, I decided to uphold it fully. I never even mock-raised my hand at my kids.

I've tried to put every tip I know that has worked for me into this book, regardless of generation and world issues. I've always believed that we need to treat our kids the way we want to be treated, with love and respect, and if you do, you will get it back. It may not happen right away, but it will - my seven decades of experiencing parenting have shown me so.

James Dudelson

January 1, 2022

PROLOGUE

I WAS RAISED by parents who helped me become independent and successful. Then I raised three independent and successful kids in two different eras. These experiences have taught me some things I would like to share with you.

I grew up in the 1950s. I became a dad to two wonderful kids in the 1980s. Then in the 2010s, in my 60s, I became a dad to another child. The world has certainly changed in that time! When I was a child I was amazed to hear my grandmother talk about growing up when most people didn't have cars. Airplanes had just been invented then and were starting to be used for travel. She told me a story about how her family drove all day (and got two flat tires) to take a trip that I can accomplish in less than an hour today.

There has been just as much change during my life. I grew up in a time when most families had cars and there were airplanes but there were no computers. Telephones were wired into the wall, and we had what was called a party line. This was a phone line that many people shared, so if you picked up the telephone, you'd sometimes hear other people talking. My grandfather bought us our first TV in 1951, but we couldn't watch it because there were no stations in Iowa where we lived. We listened to the radio.

These big changes in technology have been accompanied by major shifts in society, too. Before 1950, extended families living together was the norm: mother, father, children, grandparents, aunts, uncles, cousins. Those family members who didn't live in the same house tended to live nearby.

In the 1950s, mobility increased, and we saw the rise of the nuclear family—father, mother, and two or three children. Few women worked, especially wives and mothers. Of course, not all families were like this, but it was the norm and cultural ideal.

U.S. census data shows the change. In 1950, nearly 80% of families lived in married households. That number had declined to less than 50% by 2020. To go along with these statistics, a 2015 Pew Research Center study shows 26% of children under 18 living in households with single parents and 7% living in households with cohabiting parents. Both of those trends were sharply rising (*Parenting in America*, 2015).

Parenting styles have changed, too. Before the 1950s, the concept of parenting included rules like: children should be seen but not heard, children should be kept on a strict schedule, and don't hug and kiss your children too much.

In his 1946 book, *The Common Sense Book of Baby and Child Care*, Dr. Spock introduced the idea of parenting the individual child. He advocated that because parents know their children best, they know their children's interests and abilities, and good parenting involves paying careful attention to what each child needs at each stage of development.

These ideas were refined years later by experts like Dr. T. Berry Brazelton who, starting with his book *Infants and Mothers* in 1969, advocated that parenting be guided by the parent's understanding of their child's behavior, who the child is, and expectations based on culture and community.

But, at a fundamental level, some things about parenting have not changed. Parenting is now, as it has always been, a pillar of society. Parents protect their children's physical and emotional health. They teach their children the rules of good behavior. They model and teach values. And they nurture their children to achieve.

No parent is perfect. I'm certainly not! But parenting is a process. You learn as you go.

WHAT IS SUCCESSFUL PARENTING?

This is a question that every parent must answer. Let me tell you what successful parenting means to me. Successful parenting means helping your kids to be the best that they can be.

I have heard parents talk about wanting to make their kids happy or wealthy, or wanting their kids to have fun. These are not bad things. But, as parents, we can't make our kids happy. We can't guarantee wealth. We can give them money, but we can't guarantee they will keep it. And as every parent knows, life isn't always fun.

What we can do is teach our children how to achieve happiness, earn a living, and make time for fun themselves. We can help them learn right from wrong and help them develop the skills and habits they need to succeed.

I think it's also important to understand that, while mother and/or father are the primary influence, children also learn from the other adults in their lives. Grandparents and extended family, caregivers, friends, and neighbors all have a role to play. Parenting is a collaborative effort. Your role is to set the standards that guide all of these interactions.

When I think about successful parenting, I remember one time when I was about seven and at a birthday party. The children were playing games. My mother was watching along with the other parents while one parent led the games.

The first game was a balancing game. Each child had a piece of paper. The game leader played some music and when the music stopped the children needed to stand on the paper without touching the ground. After each round, they folded the paper into a smaller square. I lasted only three rounds. I wasn't happy—I really like to win—but I sat down and watched the rest of the game.

The next game was musical chairs. I got to the last round, but didn't win. At this point, I crawled into my Mom's lap almost in tears. She told me that she understood I wanted to win, but no one wins all the time. She told me not to cry and to buck up. She gave me a pat and told me to go back to the party because, when I cried, I made the birthday girl unhappy. I conquered my tears and enjoyed the rest of the party.

I'm sure my mother was embarrassed about me crying, but she never said anything to me. Instead, she let me know how proud of me she had been for being able to regain my self-control. I've come to recognized that these mixed feeling come with the territory of being a parent.

WHAT DO I MEAN BY SUCCESSFUL KIDS?

Successful kids are confident, happy, and kind.

They are able to go out into the world, forge strong relationships, and find satisfaction in what they do. They have the skills they need to make the most of their individual talents and abilities. They do good in the world.

My youngest son is eight. We are helping him learn to navigate the technical landscape (he really likes technology and devices), and we are proud to watch him mature and become more independent.

My two eldest kids are all grown with families of their own. It has been a joy to watch them launch themselves into the world. It hasn't always been easy.

When my son was in college and decided to major in humanities/philosophy, I was worried about his future. Today, he is a very successful entrepreneur with a wonderful wife and daughter.

My daughter, also very entrepreneurial, made her own way into the marketplace as a recruiter for a major company. She met her husband, a great guy, in college. Today they have two great children, a boy and a girl.

My children are making their way successfully through life because they have the resources to handle life's ups and downs. My goal with this book is to share the guiding principles that helped me. They can also help you successfully navigate the process that is parenting and raise successful kids.

CHAPTER 1 HOW TO SET REALISTIC EXPECTATIONS AND GOALS FOR RAISING YOUR CHILDREN

WHAT DO YOU EXPECT?

WE WANT our children to be healthy, happy, and successful. As they grow up, we want them to be well-behaved and loving.

Some parents have more specific goals in mind. They may want their child to become a doctor, lawyer, internet entrepreneur, plumber in the family business, basketball player, or Hollywood star.

Stop for a minute and ask yourself: what can I really expect from, and for, my child? What does my child want? What are my child's talents and capabilities?

Ask yourself, too, what will the world be like when my child is ready to go out on their own? That's not an easy one. Things are changing so fast, you can't be sure. In the year 2000, who would have predicted that today's students should be prepared for careers as virtual assistants, bloggers, web usability designers, web analysts, or online community managers? Not me.

In the past, people had a job and kept it for an entire career, usually with the same employer. That's changing. (*Baby boomers born from 1957 to 1964 held an average of 12.4 jobs from ages 18 to 54: The Economics Daily: U.S. Bureau of Labor Statistics*, 2021) In 2020, the U.S. Bureau of Labor Statistics reported that the average Baby Boomer, born between 1957-1964, had held more than a dozen different jobs in their career. Millennials and Gen Z-ers are likely to change jobs just as much, if not more. The statistics show that workers now tend to spend five years or less in a job.

Another telling statistic is that only 21% of college graduates report using all of their education on the job. Fifty percent of college graduates use just half or less of what they studied. And 15% don't use what they studied at all. As a result, nearly 75% of Gen X-ers expect to return to school during their working lives. Already more than 40% of college students are over 25.

Instead of having expectations and setting goals to prepare our children for a specific future, we need to focus on helping our children develop the qualities they will need to face that future.

One of the most challenging aspects of parenting in the 21st Century is the knowledge that we simply don't know what the future will bring.

As parents, we want our children to grow up to be successful, but we can't do it for them. What we can do is set expectations and goals that will help them become individuals who can achieve for themselves in a world that we cannot fully see.

WHAT QUALITIES WILL HELP YOUR CHILD SUCCEED?

How can we equip our children to make the most of their future? Education is important, and I'll talk about that in Chapter 6. In this chapter, I want to focus on key qualities they will need: **respect, self-control, perseverance, empathy, listening, and a positive attitude.** Let's consider each one.

- *Respect*

Respect starts with self-respect or a sense of self-worth.

Children who value themselves will be confident. They will expect to be treated well and respectfully. They will be able to stand up for themselves and make good choices, even in situations where making the right choice means disagreeing with their peers.

A child who has self-respect is able to value other people, too. They are better able to interact with others by being polite and kind.

How do you teach your child to respect themselves and others? As every parent knows, children need different guidance at different ages.

Babies develop self-respect from knowing they are loved, safe, and secure; and from being able to safely learn about their world. Create an environment where it is safe for your baby to touch and taste everything she can reach. Let your baby learn to do things herself. Be patient. Help her practice. When she has mastered one thing, give her something a little more challenging to do.

With toddlers and preschoolers, introduce the idea of respect for others. Teach your children good manners: to say please and thank you, and to use other people's names. Let them know that they should respond politely if someone is talking to them. Teach them to sit up at the table and ask to be excused.

I think it's important to teach our children to use titles as a sign of respect.

I had an acquaintance, Nancy, who didn't have children but who walked her dog in a neighborhood where there were lots of kids. The kids always wanted to say "hi" to the dog. When Nancy greeted them, she would say, "Hi. I'm Nancy and this is my dog, Barney." But all of the children responded by calling her "Ms. Nancy." In fact, they called all of the adults "Mr." or "Ms." Nancy told me that this made her feel old at first until she realized that the parents were teaching their children to respect the adults in their lives.

Another aspect of good manners is knowing what language to use and when. Children need to start learning this before they enter school. The slang that we all use when we are talking with family and friends makes a bad impression when talking with teachers—and, later, employers.

We all have multiple ways of speaking. We use casual language and colloquialisms with family and friends. We use more formal standard English in school at work. With friends you can say "huh," "yeah," "what's up," and "thanks." At school, your children should be able to say "what," "yes," "hello," and "thank you".

We enhance our children's self-respect when we teach them the right way to talk in different situations. They need to know when to be casual and when to be formal because formal language is the language of power. It is the language of success.

- ***Self-Control***

Self-control is about learning to recognize and deal with emotions.

From the first, babies express emotion with their voices and their faces. They start to learn to recognize emotion in their parents' and caregivers' faces and from their tone of voice. From recognizing emotions, the next step is to learn to name and control them.

Cuddle your baby. Respond when he cries. Tell him you love him. A parent soon learns that all cries are not the same. Once you recognize your baby's different cries, you know when to step in right away and when it's okay to wait. If the baby is secure in your love, he will learn how to soothe himself. This is the beginning of self-control.

Toddlers need to learn to recognize and name their own emotions. This is not easy. There's a reason people talk about the "terrible twos!" It can be frightening and confusing for toddlers to experience strong emotions but not know how to deal with them. A tantrum or meltdown is often the result.

As parents, we need to understand that when a toddler has a tantrum it is because she hasn't yet learned self-control. If she yells **"I hate you!"** it's not personal. She is learning how to name anger.

This is hard enough at home, but it can be really tough when you're out in public. You feel embarrassed and may be angry too. This is when it is especially important to teach by example.

If your toddler is having a meltdown, let him see you take a deep breath to calm yourself before you engage with him. Talk quietly or even whisper. This can be much more powerful than yelling. Your child will need to quiet himself in order to hear you. Then help him step back from the emotional storm, talk about what he feels, and suggest how to deal with those feelings. Encourage him to "Use your words."

This has been very hard for me to apply at times, as I am a natural-born yeller and can be quite emotional too. I admit that I have ended up raising my voice at times and my kids, being kids after all, started to imitate my outbursts, a behavior I realized I had to nip in the bud. So I've learnt that taking a deep breath to calm down not only works for grown-ups but for children as well.

Also notice, there will be times that your toddler looks to you to see how to feel. Children bump into things and fall down a lot. When that happens, they usually don't start to cry right away. Instead, they will look at you. If you jump up and run over, your child is likely to cry. If you say look up, smile, and say, "That's okay," they'll probably go right back to playing.

Practice is important, too. As children get older there are a lot of games that help them practice self-control: Simon Says, Freeze Dance, and Red Light, Green Light are just a few.

Psychologists also suggest a second version of Red Light Green Light that adds a more challenging element to the game. Once your child has mastered stop on red and go on green, flip the rules around. They'll have to battle their first instincts in order to stop on green and go on red, which adds a level of impulse control and makes the game much more challenging.

Beyond these specifics, we teach self-control every day when we require our children to behave well—not grabbing the package off the shelf, or walking, not running.

It is important for parents to set limits and enforce them consistently. Some limits are basic safety rules: "don't put your finger in the fire," "don't cross the road without mommy or daddy." Other limits are about regulating behavior. At bedtime, if you say "just one more story," don't read two. If you say "take two cookies," don't break down and let the kids have more (no matter how adorably they smile).

Another important part of using limits to teach self-control is to give your child choices. Choices help children learn impulse control and delayed gratification. For instance, your son asks you to play a game with him when you get home. You might say "I have time to play one game now, or we can play two games after dinner. Which would you prefer?"

We can also help our children avoid temptation which is a valuable life skill we use as adults when we need to exercise our own self-control. Before a playdate, put away a toy that you know the kids will fight over. Try not to take her past the candy aisle in the drug store if you know your daughter will want a bag of candy. Teach your children to put away phones and devices when it's time to do homework. Avoiding temptation makes self-control easier and helps set your child up for success.

I know this is easier said than done. When a child's friends come over, they always want to play with their favorite toy. Sometimes the easy choice becomes a hard one.

- ***Perseverance***

Perseverance—the ability to try, fail, pick yourself up, and try again—is an important skill for a future world of change.

Children need to persevere in order to accomplish any new or difficult task. Watch a young child with a new toy. They poke and prod and try to see what the toy will do. Then they decide they want to do something with the toy and keep trying over and over again. We call this play. It's something that young children do naturally but which becomes harder as we grow up and expect ourselves to always do things right.

Help your children learn to keep playing. Help them develop the capacity to explore and fail and keep on going. When I was little and something got tough, my parents would quote the old proverb: "If at first you don't succeed, try, try again." It was good advice.

Let your baby keep trying to put that square peg in a round hole; ultimately, she will figure it out. If your son is learning to play the guitar and is frustrated that he keeps making mistakes, don't give in to the temptation to let the screeching stop. Encourage him to keep practicing.

Perhaps your daughter wants to play soccer or your son wants to be in a play. Then she decides she doesn't want to play soccer anymore because all her friends are on a swim team or he decides the play isn't as much fun as he thought and he wants to quit. Let her know that it's okay to change her mind, but she needs to stick with it until the end of the season. Let him know that he doesn't need to be in another play if he doesn't want to, but that he needs to follow through with this one. Your daughter may make new friends. Your son may or may not want to be in another play. But in both cases, they are learning to persevere.

Also, let your children know about things you had to overcome. I don't mean "I had to walk six miles to school, barefoot, in the snow." Tell them about real challenges you had and problems you overcame. Tell them about the time you had to scramble to find a new place for your boss to hold a meeting because the room you had scheduled was taken by someone else or the time you had to reorganize work at the construction site because the drywall wasn't delivered on time. Family dinner table conversations are a natural place for these kinds of conversations.

We all have setbacks and disappointments in our lives. Our children will, too. Perseverance will help them stick with things that are difficult, solve their problems, and make it through.

- *Empathy*

Empathy has two parts: the ability to understand other people's emotions (emotional empathy) and the ability to imagine other people's points of view (cognitive empathy).

Babies start to learn emotional empathy when they learn to read your face.

You can't spoil a baby. Cuddling, watching closely, and responding right away to your baby is critical in the early months. You and the baby are getting to know each other. But cuddling and showing sympathy isn't the answer to every problem. Before your child is six, it is important to build the foundation for how they will be able to navigate in the world. As a parent you do this by helping them to develop five key characteristics:

1. the ability to control their impulses (self-control),
2. the ability to recognize and control their emotions,

3. the ability to imagine the feelings and thoughts of other people,
4. a sense of fair behavior, and
5. concern for others.

These are the components of empathy.

When your child starts to talk, you will hear her say things like "He's sad" or "She's angry." She is learning to name other people's feelings. You can use this knowledge to teach empathy.

For instance, ask your child to make a face and then tell you what it is and how it feels. If there are several children, ask one of them to make a face and the others to imagine how that feels.

You will have plenty of opportunities to teach your child empathy in the context of what they do every day.

My neighborhood is on a *cul de sac*; the children play together in the evening while we parents stand around and talk. When my son was a preschooler, he and his friend loved to play with remote control cars. Of course, both of the boys liked the red car the best.

Sometimes my son's friend would come crying to his dad that my son wouldn't let him play with the red car. I'd be a little angry, because I'd told my son he needed to share. But I knew that anger wouldn't help. So I would say to my son, "I know you want to play with the red car, but so does your friend. How would you feel if he took it away from you?"

Of course, my son still didn't want to give back the car. I had to tell him to. But only after I had gotten him to see that, when he took away the car, he made his friend feel sad.

I didn't tell my son he was bad. I didn't want him to be ashamed. Shame just makes you angry. But I did want my son to realize he had made a bad choice, to see how his actions affected his friend, to feel a little guilty for doing the wrong thing, and to be able to make amends by giving the car back.

As parents, we navigate these complicated interactions every day as we teach emotional empathy.

One powerful tool you have as a parent is to teach your children the Golden Rule: treat other people the way you want them to treat you. The Golden Rule is an idea that is easy for children to relate to. It helps them connect what they feel to what other people feel and to appreciate that the way they behave has consequences.

Developing cognitive empathy is a more intellectual exercise. Once your child has learned to understand other people's emotions, he can begin to imagine their point of view.

There was a Dutch experiment that showed the importance of cognitive empathy (Dewar, 2020). A group of more than 400 schoolchildren was split in two. Both of the groups were told about a classmate who was supposed to stay after school to clean up the classroom; the classmate needed help because her mother was sick and she wanted to go home as soon as possible. The first group was told that the classmate was a friend. The second group was not. The children were more willing to help a friend.

Then the experiment was repeated. But this time, before being asked if they would help, the children were asked to think about the classmate and rate how upset or sad she was likely to be. This time, the children did not show a bias in favor of the friend.

This kind of empathy, being able to understand and react based on how someone else might feel, is an important life skill for navigating a world of differences.

Another way children can learn empathy is from travel to other countries, other states, or other neighborhoods. Travel gives your child the opportunity to experience that people are people wherever you go.

Our world is increasingly diverse. Children naturally see things about other people that are different. Help them see what they have in common too.

Be open about biases concerning race, gender, class, wealth, and ethnicity. You can do this when you are reading together with your child and when you are talking with them about their day.

Having emotional and cognitive empathy will give your child the ability to be a better problem solver and to communicate her ideas in a way that makes sense to other people.

- ***Listening***

Listening—active listening— is another skill that will benefit your child, at school, at work, and in life.

Listening is more than being polite and not speaking when another person is talking. It is not just waiting for your turn to speak. Listening means hearing, and understanding, what the other person has to say. It requires paying attention to both words and non-verbal cues.

Children learn listening skills when you talk with them and when you read to them.

Talking with your child is an opportunity for your child to listen to you and for you to model active listening for them. Two places that I've found are great for conversations with my kids are at the family dinner table and in the car.

When you are reading to your child, ask questions about the story: "What did the Mama Bear say?" "What just happened to Harry?" "What did Pippi mean when she said that?"

There are also games that teach listening skills.

The telephone game is a fun way to experience how important listening is. You know the game. Everyone sits in a circle, the first person whispers a sentence into the ear of the person beside her, and each person in the circle repeats it to their neighbor until the last person has to listen to the sentence and repeat it out loud. The sentences always come out garbled because the players try to whisper so quietly it's hard to hear (a good lesson in itself!). But the telephone game also shows how quickly a message changes if it is not understood.

Another game that teaches listening is taking turns, one sentence at a time, to make up a story. On car trips, my kids and I used to have a lot of fun with that.

Help your child develop good listening skills by teaching them to make eye contact with someone who is talking to them, not to interrupt, and to ask questions. Asking questions shows that they are paying attention and helps them make sure they understand what is being said.

Listening is an important part of learning and an important skill for the workplace, too.

- ***Positive Attitude***

Last, but not least, is having a positive attitude. People who have a positive attitude, who think they *can*, have an easier time overcoming problems.

As parents we know that some kids have a sunny disposition, some are natural optimists, and others are more naturally negative or down. Luckily, attitude is something you can adjust.

This does not mean you should dismiss negative feelings your child may have. We all feel bad sometimes. It means you should help your child learn skills to turn bad feelings around.

If you see that your child is feeling unhappy, anxious, or down, let her know it's okay. Then help her to refocus from worrying about the problem to possible solutions.

And do your best to model a positive attitude in your life. Children learn as much, if not more, from what you do as from what you say.

There is some research that suggests that when you imitate facial expressions, your body responds as though you were actually feeling that emotion (Andrews, 2010). I think this works.

I once learned a meditation trick, in with the good air, out with the bad. You were supposed to take a deep breath in and smile on "in with the good air" and then frown as you exhaled "out with the bad". It may sound crazy, but I use the technique to this day because it makes me feel better every time.

Helping your children understand right from wrong is another way to encourage them to be positive. If your child has a clear understanding of right from wrong and follows the rules, he will have the satisfaction of knowing he's done the right thing. Guilt, doubt, and regret make it hard to have a positive attitude.

The point is, having a positive attitude will help your child deal with life's problems.

CHAPTER 2
SET UP A ROUTINE AND STICK TO IT

ROUTINES ARE a part of everyone's life—whether they were created purposefully or not.

What happens in your house at bedtime, at dinner time, or when getting out the door in the morning? At bedtime, do you spend an hour running up and down the stairs getting your child water or reading "just one more" book before she goes to sleep? You probably didn't plan it but that's a routine.

Be purposeful about the routines in your family's life and start right away. Infants thrive on routine.

As soon as they are able, get the children involved in creating routines. If the children are involved in creating the routines, they will have a sense of agency: a feeling of control over their actions and the consequences of failing to follow through.

Research backs this up. As reported in the American Journal of Lifestyle Medicine, good routines have many benefits (Arlinghaus & Johnston, 2018):

- They improve your children's ability to self-regulate, helping them recognize and master their feelings—for instance, getting out of bed on time even though they'd rather sleep in.

- The security of routines helps kids better handle the other challenges and stressors they will experience in their day.
- Routines provide a foundation for good mental health.
- Family routines are linked to the development of social skills, success in school, and the ability to handle stress.

A childhood routine is more than a schedule. It is a set of predictable, accessible rules for how to accomplish certain things. A good routine lets the child know what is expected and creates a structure in which the child participates meaningfully—whether helping to clear the table after a family meal or choosing their outfit for the day before going to bed.

It's not necessary to create a routine for every moment of your child's day. Unstructured play is important, too. The goal is to create routines that work for you and stick to them.

WHY ROUTINES MATTER

Children take comfort from the predictability and familiarity of routines. They gain confidence if they know what to expect from their day. They feel a sense of control because they know what is expected of them.

Routines also help you encourage the behavior you want your children to learn and take with them into adulthood. They create habits that help your children—and you—get everything done.

Good routines will create a secure, less stressful environment, increase your kids' confidence and self-control, promote healthy habits, and help them become more independent.

Good routines also include at least one important job the child can do. For a very young child, this might be making their own bed. As your kids get older, the jobs can be expanded to include more difficult tasks like setting and clearing the table, taking out the trash, participating in family clean-up hours, or feeding and walking the dog.

DIFFERENT KINDS OF ROUTINES

It's a good idea to have routines for the beginning and end of each day, bookending your child's day with something familiar and secure. Other routines can be useful to guide stressful or busy times—getting out the door in the morning, mealtimes, or doing household chores.

Each family is different, so routines will be different. Here are some suggestions:

Morning Routines

Morning routines help you and your child get the day off to a good start.

Morning for a toddler:

- 7:00 a.m. wake up and play in your crib
- 7:30 a.m. breakfast
- 8:00 a.m. brush teeth and get dressed
- 8:30 a.m. leave with Mom for daycare

Morning for a middle schooler:

- 6:30 a.m. wake up, get dressed, and make the bed
- 7:00 a.m. breakfast
- 7:15 a.m. make lunch while we review homework
- 7:30 a.m. leave for school

Mealtimes

Family meals are wonderful times for everyone to come together. Modern life makes it difficult for the family to all sit down together for morning and evening meals, but try to eat together at least once a day.

Family meals are a time to teach table manners. Children can help, in age-appropriate ways, to cook and clean up after meals. You can make sure your kids are having a well-rounded meal. And, you will have the joy of simply being together.

Conversations around the table help you learn about your kids' lives and help your kids learn about you.

I like to get the family together at dinner because we are all more relaxed and not getting ready to dash out the door to start the day. This is the way I was brought up. We had dinner as a family, and no matter how hungry we were we had to wait for my Dad to come home so we could all eat together. And, we never had the TV on!

If breakfast is more convenient for your family, it's more important that you all sit down together than that you do this at any particular meal or time.

Breakfast (one parent, one elementary school child, one preschooler):

- 6:30 a.m. Elementary school child gets up, gets dressed, and watches TV
- 6:45 a.m. Parent wakes preschooler and helps him get dressed
- 7:00 a.m. Everyone in the kitchen to get breakfast ready
- Elementary schooler sets the table for cereal
- Preschooler helps parent select cereal and put milk on the table
- 7:15 a.m. Children help clear table, parent washes dishes and puts lunches in backpacks
- 7:30 a.m. Children brush their teeth and get their things by the door
- 7:45 a.m. Family in the car and ready to go

Dinner (two parents, one teenager, one middle schooler):

- 6:30 p.m. Parents alternate preparing dinner while kids are doing homework or having screen time
- 7:00 p.m. Kids alternate setting table
- 7:15 p.m. Family sits down to dinner and talks about the day and other topics of mutual interest
- 7:45 p.m. Kids alternate clearing table while the parent who didn't cook loads dishwasher

Housework

Housework should be a shared responsibility. It's my philosophy that if you live here, you should help out.

Elementary School:

- Make your bed before breakfast every day (Choose bedding to make this as easy as possible. If you do so, children can start making their own beds when they start preschool.)
- Help make lunch (or, for older kids, make your own lunch) every evening before bed.
- Load the dishwasher.
- Saturday morning: vacuum and put away your laundry.

High School:

- Clean up your room before dinner on Friday (You'll notice that this rule is different from the standard "make your bed every day" rule. Teenagers often rebel against rules. They see their room as their own space. As a parent, you need to pick your battles.)
- Help wash dishes and prepare meals (this job might be shared with parents and/or siblings).
- Take out the trash on trash days.
- Saturday morning: do laundry or vacuum, dust, and pick up one room of the house. (You might let your teenager pick which room, perhaps alternating or changing every week.)

Bedtime

A bedtime routine will help your child sleep better, and give you a more pleasant evening.

Toddler:

- 6:30 p.m. Take off clothes and put them in the hamper.
- 6:35 p.m. Brush teeth and bath time (let your child choose two or three toys to play with in the tub).
- 6:50 p.m. Put on pajamas and get into bed.

- 7:00 p.m. Read a bedtime story (one or two, it's up to you, but pick a number of stories and stick with your decision).
- 7:30 p.m. Lights out.

Middle Schooler:

- 8:30 p.m. Brush teeth, shower, and get ready for bed.
- 9:15 p.m. Read or do other quiet time activities in their room.
- 10:00 p.m. Lights out.

I know it's easier said than done, but it does pay off. To set a workable, effective routine you have to keep at it each day until it becomes a habit and everyone follows the routine without thinking twice. And remember, as you set out to create routines, always allow for modifications until you find the right combination.

FAMILY RITUALS

There are also special routines, rituals, that foster a sense of togetherness and a deep sense of family identity. Rituals are different from everyday routines because they have extra meaning.

The whole family gets together at the same time and in the same place. Everyone focuses on the experience itself rather than simply completing a task.

One of the goals of a ritual is to create positive emotional bonds. These bonds will be a source of strength for your child in years to come.

We have rituals for holidays, birthdays, weddings, and funerals. These familiar rituals provide joy, celebration, and comfort at significant moments in our lives.

A vacation can be a family ritual. Perhaps your family always goes back to the same cabin at the lake each summer or always spends a week with the grandparents. Or, a family that likes to travel might plan a new adventure for each vacation.

Aside from these special occasions, your family probably also has some everyday rituals. For example, our neighbors have Friday Pizza/Movie Night. And we always stop for something to eat after one of my son's soccer games.

WHEN TO MAKE CHANGES

If you've fallen into a bad routine (for example, bedtime is not consistent or your family cannot find time to be all together), make a change. Also, make sure your routines are respectful of everyone in the house. Is there only one person cleaning, cooking, or doing the laundry? If so, change that routine.

Routines will need to change as your children grow. They may need to change when someone's school, sports, or work schedule changes.

You can also use routines to give your child the opportunity to progress. For example, your middle schooler might complain that his 9:00 p.m. curfew is way too early or much earlier than his friend's. Tell him that if he comes home by nine o'clock for the rest of the school year, you can talk about a 9:30 p.m. or 10:00 p.m. curfew in the summer.

As your kids get older, get them involved in setting their routines. If you want your daughter to get up on time, talk with her about how much sleep she needs and when she needs to go to bed. If your son is having a hard time getting up in the morning, ask him what would help: an alarm clock? a knock on the bedroom door?

Routines will also change if there's a change in the family—a divorce, a new marriage, or a new child.

In the case of divorce, if your children spend time in two different households, it's okay for routines to vary (they almost certainly will). It's not uncommon for a parent who is less present in a child's life to relax routines and try to bribe the kids with gifts, trips, or other treats. This can make it much harder to stick with your routines.

Divorced parents should make an effort to agree on some key things—but if this is not possible, follow what you know is the right way. Enforce your routines in your house while letting your children know you understand things are not the same when they are not with you. It may not seem like it when your child is angry about it, but he will understand you love him because you care enough to help him stick with the routine.

In the case of a blended family, you and your new spouse should start by agreeing on what is important. Decide the basics of what the house rules and routines will be. If parents are not on the same page, children are quite capable of playing one against the other.

Once you are in agreement, talk with the kids. Be open to their ideas about what they think the new household's routines should be. This isn't easy, but there are many resources you can find about how it can be done.

DISCIPLINE AND ROUTINES

Routines require rules, and rules require discipline.

As Dr. T. Berry Brazelton says, "Discipline is teaching, not punishment." (Brazelton and Sparrow, 2015). Discipline sets boundaries, which provide safety as the child learns to navigate the world.

For young children, it is comforting to know what will happen when you say, "It's bedtime."

For teenagers, routines offer stability when so much about their lives and themselves is changing. Knowing that her evening routine includes an 11:00 p.m. curfew can help your daughter deal with peer pressure on an evening out. She may complain "My parents are so 20th century!" but having this rule can make it easier for her when she wants to say "No" to her friends.

My parents had a strict rule when I was a High School senior: curfew at 11:45. If I were going to be later (not longer than a half-hour), I would have to call at 11:30 and let them know, and I would have to call each time I wanted to extend my curfew by 15 minutes. I had to carry a lot of dimes with me; there were only payphones available back then.

Each routine should include expectations: lights out by 9:00 p.m. or beds made before breakfast. And the kids should know that if expectations are not met, there will be appropriate consequences. It's your job as a parent to know your children, know what they understand and are capable of, and set realistic expectations for them at every age.

For example, part of the routine for your 10-year-old son may be to put his iPad away by plugging it into the house charging station by 7:30 p.m. for homework time. Let him know that if he doesn't there will be no screen time the next day.

If your teenager is supposed to put the laundry away by supper time on Saturday, the consequence might be that she can't do anything else after dinner until the job is done. So, if on Saturday night your daughter wants to go out with a friend but the laundry has not been put away, let her know that she can't go out until the job is done.

Of course, you can't win every battle. Know when it's time to try a different approach. For example, did you give your daughter the command to "go to bed" which resulted in an argument? You may choose to avoid a pitched battle by letting bedtime slide this time. Next time, try saying "It's time for bed," and see if you get a better result.

CHAPTER 3
BE INVOLVED IN YOUR KID'S LIFE

BE PRESENT FOR YOUR CHILD. This means more than just physical presence, it means being involved in a positive way. Even when you are not there, you can be that voice in their head—the angel on their shoulder—that counters the voice of temptation. You are helping them form principles to carry with them to guide them in making choices.

I know of a young girl, Janet, who was an only child of divorce. Both her mother and step-father worked, and her step-father cooked the evening meal. Each morning before he left for work, her step-father would make a list of what food he needed for dinner that night. He left the list along with a pile of money on the kitchen table.

After school, Janet took the list to the corner store to buy what was needed. Any money that was left over she could keep. This kept Janet busy while her parents were still at work and made a game of her helping out. Janet was never particularly close to her step-father but she was always grateful for that thoughtfulness.

We live in a busy world. In many families—in single-parent households and in nearly 60% of two-parent households—parents who work full time are challenged to be physically present for their children as much as they would like. But by creating the voice of conscience in your children's head, you can be involved even when you're not there.

BUILD A CLOSE RELATIONSHIP

A close relationship with their parents is the strongest predictor of a child's future success, according to a recent Harvard study (Popomaronis, 2019). Here are some strategies that have worked for me.

Keep Your Kid's Point of View in Mind

Remember that the things that concern you often don't really matter to your child. You want to be on time. Little kids don't know or care what time it is. You want your kids to be clean and well-behaved. They revel in being dirty and sticky. You want the house to be neat and clean. Your toddler doesn't notice and your teenager loves a room in chaos.

Ask your daughter to tell you, and show you, about things she likes. Talk with your son about things that interest him. Try to make time if they ask you to play. Children have short attention spans. The play session may be less than 15 minutes but it shows that you care.

Rather than force your kids to think as you do, look for ways to relate what you want to something that matters to them. We've probably all turned the spoon into an airplane to land food in our infant's mouth. This technique doesn't stop working just because your children grow.

For the toddler who doesn't want to calm down so you can put on his shirt, try turning getting dressed into play. Make his clothes talk: "I'm a kite but I want to be a shirt. Isn't there a little boy I can land on?"

For the teenager who likes a messy room, keep in mind that teenagers are eager for more control in their life, and they think of their room—or their part of the room—as their space. If your teenager has a room of her own, relax your clean up every day rule for her, tell her you trust her and won't supervise her, ask her to keep the door closed (she may already be doing this!), and explain that she is expected to clean up by a certain time once a week. Give her a choice: Does she want to have her room clean by Friday night or Saturday lunchtime?

Tell Personal Stories

Children are self-centered. It's natural. And, they love stories.

Young children will ask you time and again for stories about themselves. "What was I like when I was a baby?" And you can ask them, "Do you remember when...?"

Kids also like to hear stories about you when you were little, stories about their grandparents, and about their family history. While stories in books will help your child forge connections with the wider world, stories about family help your child build a strong sense of self and their place in the world. Simply being together and sharing these stories will bring you closer.

Young children are especially interested in family stories. Teenagers, who are focused on their peers, may not seem as interested but they will remember. Telling and re-telling these stories can be a treasured part of family occasions.

Be There

When our children start to go out into the world, we need to find other ways to stay involved in their lives and maintain a close relationship.

Be there for important events. If your son is on a basketball team, attend his games. If your daughter is learning to play piano, attend her recitals. If your child is involved in Scouting or 4-H, attend events. See if there is some way you can volunteer.

Be involved at your child's school. Go to back-to-school night to meet the teacher. Participate in the parent teacher association (PTA). Attend school carnivals and science fairs. Attend major school-wide events like the holiday concert even if your child is not performing.

I know that some parents have multiple jobs, or jobs with inflexible schedules, and being present for these events is simply not possible. In that case, talk with your child. Explain that you wish you could be there and how sorry you are that you can't. Your child already knows how hard you work. Make sure they also know that you are aware of what's going on in their life and that you care. Afterward, ask them to tell you about it.

Does it sometimes seem that the only way you're there for your kid is to be a chauffeur? Driving kids around can seem like a chore but it's a wonderful window into your child's life. The carpool driver will learn a lot from what the kids tell each other.

Just as they think the teacher doesn't know what's going on in the classroom, children don't consider the listening ears of the carpool driver. So you will hear about what's going on in your kid's life, and that can be a great conversation starter later on.

If it's just you and your child in the car, this can be a great time to talk. There are no distractions for the child, the child can't physically go away, the distraction of driving helps you keep a lid on emotions, and there's less pressure because you and your child are not making constant eye contact.

When you are talking, practice—and model—active listening. Ask open-ended but specific questions. Instead of "How was school?" ask "What happened in science class today?" If your child tells you about a problem, don't jump right in with advice about how to solve it. Instead, ask something like "What do you think you can do?" or "Would you like to hear what I would do?" If they say no, that's okay.

Know your child's friends and their parents. As they get older, they may complain about this. But it shows how much you care.

If your child is going out, know where they are going, who else is going, and what they plan to do. Ask, if you don't know. When they get back, ask how it went: What happened? What was your favorite part...? How is John, or Mary, doing…?

Be a mentor. Mentoring isn't teaching, it's guiding, it's understanding, and bringing out the best in your child.

Provide a varied, stimulating environment when your child is young. See what interests him and nurture those interests. Perhaps your son has books, Legos, action figures, trucks, and videos to play with. You see that he especially likes to put on videos and dance along to the music. Instead of trying to get him to play with the other toys, ask if he'd like to take a music, Tae Kwan Do, or dance class.

Keep the Lines of Communication Open

You can't—and shouldn't—promise not to be upset. But you can promise to listen to your child and respect what she says. You can promise to keep a confidence.

If you have more than one child, you will probably find that one child is more talkative and the other more private. Respect these differences. When your son is bubbling over with enthusiasm for how the game went, listen and enjoy. If you can tell that your daughter is upset but she doesn't want to talk about it, tell her that you are there, ready to listen when she wants to talk.

One of the big reasons that I am such a strong advocate for family meals is that so much conversation happens around the dining table.

WHY IT IS IMPORTANT TO HAVE A STRONG, POSITIVE BOND WITH YOUR KID

This may seem like a no-brainer: parents want strong, positive bonds with their children. Research backs this up (Lee & Lok, 2012).

Babies are totally dependent on their parents. They start to bond while you hold them in your arms—feeding, soothing, and simply cuddling them. Their brain development, social, emotional, and cognitive development all depend on a loving bond with a parent. This is crucial in the first two years of life.

As children grow, it's up to you to relate to them in ways that encourage and strengthen these bonds. Listen to them. Respect their feelings. Hold them to important standards of good behavior. Show them your love, no matter what happens.

Strong positive bonds with you benefit your child in many ways:

- Repeated loving interactions help lay down pathways in the brain that support the formation of memory and enhance the development of learning and logic.
- Your child will develop good language and emotional skills.
- Your child is more likely to become happy, resilient, and independent.
- Your child will have a greater ability, throughout their life, to form and sustain healthy relationships.
- Your child will have better mental health and be better able to cope with stress.
- They will have higher self-esteem, self-confidence, self-control, social competence, problem-solving ability, and a greater capacity to make friends.
- A strong bond with your adolescent will help your child be better socialized, form healthy attachments to peers, and avoid risky and illegal behavior.

This bond also benefits you:

- Strong, positive bonds with your children are the basis of a happy family.
- You are able to model and teach strong ethics and moral values.
- Your child will be better able to avoid risky behaviors related to sex, drug use, and violence, no matter the family structure.
- Your children will enjoy spending time with you, both now and when they are grown.

SPEND TIME WITH YOUR KIDS AND MAKE IT FUN

If both parents work long hours, it can be tempting to focus on always having fun together when you are with your child. Fun is important, and you can find it in many ways. Yes, play with them when you can. Go to the movies. Yet, in addition, look for ways to involve them in what you do.

Family Time

You often hear about the importance of maintaining a good work-life balance. Parents especially can struggle with this. Being involved in your kid's life means trying to be home on time, keeping work at work, and learning how to turn off office emails.

I consider that family time happens whenever the parent is home and the kids are in the house. This is true even when they're not in the same room. My kids always knew that I was aware of where they were and what they were doing.

Family time includes daily routines and the many opportunities you have to interact with each other.

Pay attention to the things your kids like to do. This shows that you care.

Try to involve your kids in things you love to do. If you like to run, can your son run with you, at least once in a while? If you like to read, perhaps you can read a book together with a younger child or simply read in the same room with your older child.

Children want to be more independent as they get older, but they do still want and need you. Strike a balance between encouraging their independent activities and including them in family activities. There may be a time in the teenage years when it seems that family rituals are the only times the whole family is together. Don't complain. Enjoy the time.

Quality vs. Quantity

You always hear these days about how important it is to spend "quality time" with your kids. Often this is expressed in terms of taking them to amusement parks or out to dinner. Yes, these things can be fun, quality experiences. But not always.

If you take the kids to an amusement park but spend the whole day yelling at them because they are being rowdy, is this quality time?

You may want to go out to dinner, but is simply taking your kids to a restaurant the same as spending quality time with them?

Years ago, I was in a restaurant with my mother. Beside us was a young family: mom, dad, and two kids of about 8 or 10. As my mother and I were talking, I noticed how quiet it was at the table beside us. When I looked over, both parents were busy with their phones. The kids were just sitting there. I hope those parents didn't think they were spending quality time with their kids!

Yes, quality time can include fun and games. It also means including your child in the business of family life.

Help your children understand that the family has a budget. Explain this in age-appropriate ways that make sense to them. For example, it's okay to tell your youngster that your budget allows for one bag of cookies, not two. Ask them which cookies to get. Let your teenager know how much money they can spend on new clothes for school. Then help them make good spending decisions.

And yes, by including your child in the business of family life, I also mean chores!

When your child is a toddler, take advantage of the toddler's desire to do what you are doing. Let him help with vacuuming, let her help with cooking—even though it may be easier and quicker to do the job yourself.

Once they know what to do and how to do it, the housework will get done much more quickly. You will have more time to be involved in your kids' lives in other ways. And if you all work together—for instance, getting together as a family to do chores on Saturday morning—it teaches your kids how to work together and fosters a sense of family camaraderie.

I believe that household chores should be a part of your kid's life from the beginning—starting from when they can walk and talk. As soon as they are able to get toys out, they can help put them away. As they grow, ask them to handle new tasks that are age-appropriate.

Did you grow up in a family where it was the parents' job to make money and take care of the house, and the children's job was school? It doesn't have to be that way. Everyone lives in the house together and should share in the responsibility. If it didn't start out that way, this can be difficult to change—but you can!

CHAPTER 4
ENCOURAGE THEM TO BE INDEPENDENT

WHEN I WAS A CHILD, we used to go outside and play on our own. At first, the rule was: Stay in the yard. Then: Don't cross the road. By the time we were seven or eight, we were playing all over the neighborhood. Once we hit middle school, we roamed all over town. In the summer, we would leave the house in the morning, dropping into one house or another for lunch or snacks, and not go home until the sun went down.

The world is different now and so childhood is different, too. For instance, in the 1950s, I walked three miles to school. Yet in the 1980s, we drove our kids to school, as we do now with my youngest.

Has the world become a more dangerous place? Without a doubt. Things that were safe fifty years ago simply aren't safe today.

This presents a challenge. You want to raise your kids to be independent. But when all you see when you look out the window is fear, there is no beneficial growth or development.

How can you teach your kids to be independent in the world today?

BOLSTER THEIR SELF-CONFIDENCE

One important way to help your child learn how to be independent is to strengthen his sense of self-confidence.

Start small and take it in steps:

- Let your infant poke and prod, taste and touch—all while keeping a careful watch to be sure he doesn't hurt himself.
- As he grows, let him play in another room with a friend at your house, then take him for a playdate at the friend's house.
- When your daughter asks to go on a sleepover, let her try. She may cry to come home the first time, but let her try again when she is ready.
- Teach her how to cross the street.
- Let him go on outings with friends (as long as you know the family and know where they will go!).
- Soon, your teenager will be ready to date and drive.

At each step of the way, your children are learning to cope with new things and developing the confidence that they can handle them.

We learn from experience. Let your daughter do things for herself as much as possible. Pay attention and offer guidance if it is needed. Step in to keep her safe. Be ready to help. But only offer to help if it is really necessary. For example, you would never let your toddler put her hand on a hot oven burner, but she can learn from experience not to touch the hot oven door again.

Give Your Kids Opportunities to Make Choices.

Too many choices can be overwhelming. This is borne out by research that measures a fear response in the cardiovascular systems of people who are making choices—especially if they fear making the wrong decision (Saltsman, 2019). So when you are helping your kid learn to make choices, be aware that a choice that seems simple to you may matter a lot to him.

Start when they are young by offering just two options. When your daughter is getting dressed, ask, "Would you like to wear the blue dress or the red dress?" If your son is with you in the grocery store ask him, "Should we buy apples or peaches today?"

Getting dressed in the morning is a good opportunity to help your kid learn to be self-confident and make good choices. Teach young kids to dress themselves. Let them do it and choose what to wear. Yes, you will have to guide these choices until they learn what's appropriate. But the standard should be what's appropriate, not what you like.

And pick your battles. I have a friend whose three-year-old son is proud of being able to dress himself, but he insists on wearing his shoes on the wrong feet. Does this bother his mom? Yes. Does it hurt his feet? No. The arch of the foot isn't developed in a three-year-old. So sometimes mom helps him put his shoes on the right feet, but she doesn't all the time.

From Choices to Decisions

As your kids get older, help them continue to learn by framing decisions that are more complex. Make an explicit connection between a decision and its consequences: "If you help me clean up, we'll have time to play before bed." or "Ask nicely and she will be more likely to listen to you."

Making these more complex decisions involves solving a problem. The child who wants to play when his mother needs to clean up, faces a problem: How can I get mom to play? By framing a choice that meets both her needs and his, mom can help her son make a good decision. And, solving problems by making good decisions is part of developing self-confidence.

ENCOURAGE PARTICIPATION AND EXPLORATION

Encourage your kids to participate in activities they enjoy. It doesn't matter whether this is taking an art class, playing sports, or joining the math club. Your kid may want to try it all! Let him.

Participating in a variety of activities provides your child with a well-rounded experience. It is a way for her to explore her capabilities in different environments. The more she accomplishes, the greater her self-confidence. The more self-confident, the more independent she will be.

Also, encourage your kids to try new things. This may mean encouraging a young artist to give swimming or gymnastics a try or encouraging a young athlete to learn a musical instrument. They may find they like it, they may not. But either way, they have learned something new.

Knowing about something, even on the most basic level, contributes to your child's understanding of the world.

Marian Wright Edelman famously said, "It's hard to be what you can't see." She was talking about diversity and the importance of inclusion (Edelman, 2015). I think her words also have meaning in terms of the importance of a child's scope of experience.

Trying new things introduces children to new capabilities within themselves and new possibilities in their world.

Trying new things usually includes an element of risk. As a parent, your instinct is to protect your child, but learning how to take risks is part of becoming independent.

Encourage healthy risk-taking through unstructured play. What do I mean by healthy risk-taking? I mean creating opportunities for your child to push herself a little and explore her limits.

Let your toddler run fast when he is inside on a carpet or outside on the grass. Yes, he will fall but you have minimized the risk he will be hurt. Let your daughter climb the tree, and be ready if she calls you to help her get down.

These experiences are part of how children learn the limits of their abilities and their world.

TEACH THEM WHAT THEY NEED TO KNOW TO BE SAFE

If your children are going to become independent, they also need to know how to be safe. Make them aware of potential dangers without making them afraid.

It is impossible to shield your child from hearing about frightening things in the world: terrorism, natural disasters, or mass shootings. Some children grow up in neighborhoods where crime is an everyday danger. All school children these days practice locking down in the event of a school shooting incident.

In the 1950s, we practiced what we would do in the case of a nuclear bomb. Luckily, the nuclear threat never materialized. Today, there is no denying the truth that school shootings can happen. They are still highly unlikely, but your child still needs to be prepared.

Just as you taught your baby by protecting her from hurting herself, you can teach your growing child important safety information.

As soon as she can speak, teach her to say and spell her name—first and last. You can make this a game, even before she knows the alphabet.

As soon as he is able, teach him his address and your cell phone number. Teach him how and when to call 911.

Teach them about stranger danger. Teach them how to recognize behavior that is inappropriate from someone they know and what to do about that. There are many resources with good advice about how to do this.

Teach young children not to go anywhere, even with someone they know, if they do not have your permission. Make sure they know they should tell you any time they feel uncomfortable or uncertain.

Teach your children to respect themselves and others. When they reach the age to start dating, teach your sons to respect girls and to behave like a gentleman. Teach your daughters to respect boys and behave in a way that demands respect in return.

TEACH THEM ABOUT MONEY

It is not easy to teach children about money, especially if you struggle with money issues yourself. But learning how to handle money is an important skill children need to achieve independence.

If your budget allows, consider giving your kid an allowance. It can be a good way to teach them about how to manage money.

Give your child an amount that is affordable and age-appropriate, meaning enough for them to be able to buy things they might want. Twenty-five cents a week is probably enough for a youngster who just wants to buy cookies or candy. A preschooler who also wants toys may get one to five dollars. Ten or twenty dollars might be appropriate for an older child who wants more expensive things.

There are many options for how to handle an allowance. Here are a few:

- With an open-ended allowance, you simply give your child an agreed-upon amount of money every week or month. Then it's up to your kid to decide what he wants to do with the money.
- Rather than give your child money each week, you might prefer an allowance, or allowances, of money they can spend for specific things, such as their own phone, or clothes for the new school year. (You may want a clothing allowance to include rules for what is appropriate, too.)
- In some families, the child is required to save a portion of each allowance either in a savings or investment account. Kids need to learn how to save. They will want to make expensive purchases someday, like a car or a house. In retirement, they won't be able to rely on pensions, or perhaps even Social Security, so they'll need to save for the future, too.
- It is not a good idea to make an allowance payment for helping out around the house, but household chores can be a source of added income for your child. If there are jobs that you would pay for and that your kids would be able to do, consider making a list of these, each with a dollar amount. Then if your child wants extra money for something beyond the scope of his allowance, he can do one or more of these jobs to raise the funds. This strategy is especially useful for kids who are too young to get a job outside the home.

Having an allowance helps children learn about managing resources, working within limits, and dealing with delayed gratification.

My friend Dan gives his kids "tips" instead of an allowance: they earn money by completing tasks he sets for them beyond the list of house chores they need to do. For example, it might be a grocery run or helping pack boxes to take to the post office.

If you can't afford a cash allowance, or give them money tips, there are other options for teaching these lessons.

For example, you are well aware of the many things your kids need. Food, housing, phone, transportation, clothes, haircuts, school supplies, and more. All of these things cost money. Even if you do not have a conversation about the family budget, your children know in general what the money situation is. So don't make it a secret.

When your kids are old enough to start asking you to buy them things, talk with them about what things cost. Explain what a budget is and how important it is to handle money responsibly.

If your child wants something that is too expensive—even if you could stretch and afford it—it's okay to say, "No, we are not going to buy that." Or if the specific brand they want is crazy expensive but there are other options, discuss those. You are teaching your child an important lesson about setting priorities and managing money.

There are two other important lessons your child needs to learn about money: how to handle credit, and how to handle the pressure of the media.

Credit cards are very useful. They are taking the place of cash for everyday transactions. But it is all too easy to fall into dangerous credit debt.

Don't give your child a credit card unless it has a spending limit. And, make that limit something you can afford to pay in full every month. In fact, don't use a credit card, use a debit card.

It's possible to set up a card that automatically deposits an allowance at the intervals you select. Your kids can personalize their cards. You can elect to put a set amount on the card at regular intervals. You can elect to have a portion of the amount deposited into your kid's savings account. And, if you'd like, you can get real-time notifications whenever the card is used.

Unrealistic media expectations are one of the primary reasons children will be tempted to overspend on credit. Advertising is one problem. A constant bombardment of ads entices kids, who have no concept of the value of money, to want things no matter the cost. A more subtle, but equally damaging, problem is unrealistic media portrayals of economic realities. The costumes and sets in popular media convey false economic messages—teaching children to want things they do not need and cannot afford.

One prime example is the popular TV show from the 1990s, Friends. The Greenwich Village apartment where the friends gathered cost far more than 20-something young professionals could have afforded. The show came up with a reason the kids could afford to live there, but who remembers that? Kids who watched the show uncritically simply thought living like that should be possible for them, too.

It is important to teach your children to be critical media consumers if they are to successfully navigate in the real world.

TECHNOLOGY

Internet technology presents a new challenge for parents—a challenge that is compounded by the fact that kids (digital natives) are often more facile with using technology than we are.

It seems that each generation has to deal with this problem. Earlier generations of parents asked: How much TV is too much? Should I let my kids listen to Elvis or the Beatles?

My mother was worried about how fascinated her grandchildren were with cell phones, but then she found a photo of my sister when she was very young playing like she was talking on the family's dial-up telephone. The truth is, we are fascinated by computers and smartphones and, because we are, our children are, too.

Computers and smartphones are valuable tools. Kids want them. To be independent, they need to learn how to safely use them.

Limit access and use, just as you do with videos or sugary treats. You want to teach your kids how to use technology just as you teach them how to eat a healthy diet or balance school and play.

It is critical that you lead by example. How can you discourage your child from being glued to her phone 24/7 when that's what she sees you do?

As your children get older and start to visit their friends' houses, talk with them about how those families handle technology. Reinforce your rules and explain again why they are important.

Make it a practice in your family to put technology away at the end of every day. Have a central place where everyone puts their devices, turns them off, and recharges.

When they are young, you can get them devices with strong parental controls. But as they get older they will venture independently onto the web. Teach them how to surf the web safely and responsibly.

Tell them about dangers like cyber-bullying, cyber-stalking, and phishing. Tell them how to protect themselves. Together, watch videos about these problems and talk about what you see. Show your kids how criminals mask their identity.

It's challenging because kids think they are invulnerable. Appeal to their sense of pride by telling them how they can be smarter than the bad guys.

Here are some suggested guidelines for teaching your kids how to be safe:

- Tell them to check with you before they share personal information.
- Get your permission to join a website or create an avatar or account on a website.
- Have regular check-ins where you review their privacy settings and they can share their online activities and interests with you.

PARTICIPATE AS MUCH AS YOU CAN—AND SHOULD

Positive parental involvement is an important part of a child's success. The question is: How much should we be involved?

When your child is an infant, it's easy. They need you every day in every way. As they grow up, you need to pull back. In order to develop independence, your child needs to learn to do things without you.

Here are some signs that you may be over-involved in your child's life:

- Do you have constant power struggles?

- Are you always trying to make your child do things "the best way" or "the right way?"
- Do you always step in to prevent your child from making mistakes?
- Do you often argue with caregivers or teachers about how your child is being treated?
- Do you avoid giving your child jobs or responsibilities?

In order to learn to be independent, children need to learn how to make choices, learn from mistakes, experience different expectations in different environments, and accept and meet responsibilities. Over-parenting prevents your children from learning these important lessons.

Two examples of over-parenting are the "Tiger Mom" and the "Helicopter Parent".

The term "Tiger Mom" was coined by Amy Chua in her 2011 book, *Battle Hymn of the Tiger Mother*. The book describes Chinese methods of raising successful kids. It is a strict, emotionally unsupportive parenting style. It assumes that children are strong, not weak, and holds them to very high standards. A Tiger Mom thinks an A- is a failure. She requires her child to learn either the piano or violin.

Tiger parenting deliberately counters the permissiveness of American culture, but it can be cruel.

Parents do need to set expectations and limits. Children do need to learn perseverance, how to practice, and work hard. There are stories about Tiger Moms with successful kids, but research shows that more supportive parenting gets better results overall (Chamberlin, 2013).

Helicopter Parents also want to control every aspect of their children's lives but, unlike the Tiger Mom, they are not sure their child can succeed. The Tiger Mom expects her child can succeed and pushes him to do so. Helicopter Parents aren't sure their child can succeed and rush in to prevent failure.

Helicopter parenting is overprotective to the point that children become dependent on their parents, stay dependent as they age, and develop all sorts of fears about the world. At its extreme, helicopter parenting can create a child who needs expert intervention from a psychologist or therapist in order to achieve independence.

Also, children who grow up expecting special treatment will have a hard time adjusting to the real world. I've had experience with these grown children in the workplace where they struggle to meet basic job expectations.

If you try to protect your child from experiencing failure, you will prevent them from learning how to jump back in and try again. They will not learn resilience which is a critical life skill.

It takes resilience to keep trying until you reach your goal. How many famous actors have you heard interviewed, after they became an overnight success, responding with stories about the many years they auditioned and tried.

FOCUS ON ACTIONS, NOT FEELINGS

Finally, an important but often unmentioned part of learning to be independent is learning that how you act can be more important than how you feel.

We can't stop ourselves from having feelings. What we can control is how we act.

Children experience storms of feeling. This is why toddlers have tantrums and teenagers act out. Our job as parents is to help our children learn how to bring their feelings under control. Whether positive or negative, we need to learn how to recognize and name what we feel, acknowledge the feelings, and master them.

You can start teaching your children this right away. "Yes, I understand that you are scared, but crying won't make you feel better." "I know it made you angry when Joey took your toy, but hitting him is not a good way to respond."

I'm sure you've heard the saying "Fake it 'til you make it." This dynamic is real. Sometimes, in order to be a responsible, independent adult, your child will need to overcome negative emotions and simply do the job. As an adult holding down a job, your child will need to go to work and do her best, even when there are difficult things happening in her life and no matter how this makes her feel.

CHAPTER 5
FIND WAYS FOR YOUR KIDS TO BE PART OF THE COMMUNITY

WHEN OUR CHILDREN ARE YOUNG, we let them know they are part of a larger community by telling them stories about what it was like when we were growing up and about their family history.

Then they start going out into the world and their community expands. They get to know the people in the building and on your street. They meet friends and their friends' families. They meet people in shops, in church, and in school. And they start to hear about things that happen to other people all over the world.

All of these relationships and experiences help your child grow, enhancing their emotional and intellectual development.

IT TAKES A VILLAGE TO RAISE A KID

One thing every parent learns is that you can't raise a kid all alone. We've all heard the African proverb, "It takes a village." This doesn't just mean that you will need help. It's also that the whole community benefits from raising children well.

I recently saw a video about the traditional greeting of the African Masai tribe. Instead of saying "Hello," the warrior's greeting is "And how are the children?" The response is, "All the children are well." Because, when a community is healthy, the children are well.

Let your child get to know the community. Let the community get to know your child. Visit parks and museums and, when appropriate, engage with people you meet.

Create social networks that help your child understand that these relationships go both ways. The important thing here is to encourage them, not to force them. Finding our community spirit is a personal discovery.

My youngest son went through a phase in which he really could not relate to anyone outside of our family circle. Neighbors and close friends alike would greet him, and he'd only stare back or look away. Not in fear, though. It seemed to me my son was negotiating how he felt about the people around us - were they like family? Could they be like family? Although I insisted he remained polite, I never forced him to shake a hand or receive a kiss if he felt uncomfortable. Then, I noticed how he slowly started to make up his mind about people and greet them warmly, often offering to help out if needed. Another way to forge community bonds for an older child is mentorship. A mentor is someone who can help your child achieve a certain goal.

Your daughter may want to learn about being a movie producer. Do you know anyone in that field? If not, you can help her reach out to a local TV station or production company and ask if she can meet with someone who works there. If your daughter is young, it's a good idea to contact the person or organization first to make sure they have the time and interest to meet with your daughter. If she is old enough, you can show her how to reach out on her own.

Your son may be growing up in a single-parent home and need the benefit of an adult man in his life. Boys and Girls Clubs and other mentoring organizations offer role models and support.

Kids can help their mentors, too. Many children are much better than adults at technology, for example. In a less tangible way, getting to know your child helps the mentor get to know the next generation.

CREATE A SENSE OF CIVIC DUTY

Our children need to grow up to have a sense of civic duty and responsibility—to know and adhere to things that are expected from everyone in our society.

It will be their civic duty one day to pay taxes, serve on juries, and obey the law. This includes everything from criminal laws to the laws of the road. If drivers don't obey traffic laws, there would be chaos on the roads. People get hurt and die when individuals ignore criminal laws.

Children also need to learn about civic responsibilities—other things they will do to be a good citizen—like voting and volunteering. Take them with you when you go to vote. Make volunteering a family project.

Many of these lessons will be taught in school. They are also taught by your example.

Ben Franklin is famously remembered as saying, upon ratification of the Constitution, that we have a republic if we can keep it. Keeping it requires citizens who are educated, law-abiding, and involved.

FIGHT SELF-ENTITLEMENT

A self-entitled child is one who thinks she should always get her way. He is one who believes he deserves everything good in life without any effort on his part. We see examples of this behavior everywhere, from the recent college admissions scandals to the lack of ability to compromise that is crippling our political system.

What can you do to fight self-entitlement in your child? Here are five strategies to use:

1. Give your child the basics, but don't give them too much. If your son needs sneakers, don't be sucked into the brand name trap. There are plenty of options that don't cost hundreds of dollars. If your daughter wants a car, is she

really ready for one unless she can pay at least some of the cost herself?

2. Let your child experience the consequences of mistakes and bad choices. Start early when the consequences are relatively minor.
3. Help your child understand responsibility and that they can't win everything all the time. The trend in competitive children's sports to award trophies for just being there can falsely boost your child's self-esteem. Being there is their basic responsibility.
4. Don't give in to bad behavior and don't let them always have their way.
5. Encourage good citizenship. At home, this means helping out around the house. Outside the home, it means behaving well and following the rules.

The struggle against self-entitlement can be harder if you have an only child. He won't have any siblings with whom he can learn to compromise and share. So if you are raising an only child, it is especially important for you to have clear expectations with consequences he knows in advance. Then, follow through.

COMMUNITY PROGRAMS AND ACTIVITIES

Being part of the community, giving back, is a chance for your child to put empathy into action. Volunteering and participating in community programs are great ways to teach your child about giving back to the community. Here are just some possibilities:

Donate to Charity

Children get a lot of things and they outgrow them quickly. Talk with your child about the difference between wants and needs. Once or twice a year, you and your child can go through your child's closet and shelves. Help them select things that they have outgrown or do not need any more. Do the same in your own closet. Then go together to take the donations to Goodwill or another charity.

Animal shelters are always glad to get donations of lightly used towels and dog toys.

Birthday Party Donations

Does your daughter like to have large birthday parties with lots of guests? That's great, but does she really need a dozen or more presents? If you are having a party with lots of guests, ask the guests to bring gifts that will be donated to a charity of your child's choice. When you are planning the party, you and your daughter can investigate different charities and decide what types of gifts will be needed. You might consider clothes and toys for kids, books to donate to a family shelter, or kitchenware to donate to a Habitat for Humanity house.

Hold a Fundraiser

If your child feels strongly about a cause or charity, talk with them about what they might be able to do. Can they raise money by asking for donations in the community or by running a lemonade stand?

Volunteer

There are lots of opportunities for you and your child to volunteer. You might:

- help in a food kitchen,
- contribute non-perishables to a local food bank, or
- participate in a clean-up day at the local park.

Support the Troops

Several organizations provide guidance for ways your child can support our active and retired military personnel. These include sending a care package, writing a card or letter, and raising money for local veteran's organizations.

Holiday Giving

At Christmas, some malls have a tree with names of families in need. You can pick a card from the tree and put together a Santa's bag of gifts that will appeal to each member of the family.

Share Their Talent

If your kid sings or plays an instrument, many senior communities have opportunities to perform for the residents.

Help a Neighbor

You may have an elderly neighbor nearby who needs help or perhaps someone who is disabled or otherwise in need. Your child might be able to carry in groceries, rake the leaves, mow the lawn, shovel snow, or walk the dog. Your youngster might simply draw them a picture or make them a card.

Disaster Relief

When your child hears news about a disaster—a hurricane, wildfire, or tsunami—she may want to do something to help. Talk with her about what she thinks might be needed. Then contact one of the support groups actually helping on the ground to find out what is needed most.

CHAPTER 6
ENCOURAGE YOUR KIDS TO BE INVOLVED IN THEIR EDUCATION

WHEN I PICK up my 8-year-old from school, the first thing we do is get him a snack and a glass of milk. Then he does his homework. He has a 20-minute break. Then we review the homework, and we work on an advance schedule for any upcoming exams that week. If he has a spelling test on Friday, we start working on it on Tuesday. Without a consistent routine, my youngest simply loses focus.

My older kids, on the other hand, were very self-motivated. I kept our routines very simple as they were good at sticking to their own goals.

Each child's needs are different. But there are things that every child does need: encouragement and the right attitude.

Research shows that student learning outcomes correlate directly to the students' sense of control over their own learning (Ed.D, 2018). The more a student believes that his actions have the power to influence outcomes, the better he will do.

To succeed in school, children need what psychologist Carol Dweck calls a "growth mindset" (mindsetworks.com, 2017)

A growth mindset is the belief that, because your brain grows, it is possible to get smarter and that working harder will pay off. Professor Dweck's work focused on what teachers can do to foster this mindset in their students. But parents have the power to encourage this mindset too.

You probably won't teach your kids about brain neuroscience. You can express your confidence in them, help them learn good study habits, and encourage them to invest time and effort into their education.

The ability to develop a growth mindset is especially important for children who have been influenced by culture or other factors to believe that things are stacked against them. The fact is, sometimes the world does put obstacles in a child's way due to their ethnicity, their gender, or perceptions about their native intelligence. In these situations, it is more important than ever to encourage children to believe in their ability to achieve.

A story on the TV show *CBS Sunday Morning* is a case in point. It showcased a man who was born without arms and who has become one of the best archers in the world—competing against fully-abled people. This happened because he was talented. But it wouldn't have happened if his parents hadn't encouraged him to believe that he could.

PREPARING YOUR PRESCHOOLER

Words

Read to your child. Cuddling together while you read is a bonding experience and an excellent way to help prepare your child to learn. Stories help kids learn about the world. Listening to stories builds vocabulary and develops listening and comprehension skills.

As you read together, use questions to help them understand. With picture books, ask what your child sees in the picture before you read the page. Or ask, "Why do you think the mother's face is red?" With storybooks, ask your child what he thinks will happen next or what she thinks about what has happened.

Relate what you read in books to what you see in real life: "Look, that's a fire engine, just like in "What's Up, Fire Truck?"

You can teach your child the alphabet using letter toys and the alphabet song. But no, your child does not need to know the alphabet, or how to read, before she starts school. Your job as a parent is to help her be ready to learn.

Numbers

For some reason, we have a cultural bias against numbers and math. Girls, especially, are often taught that they're simply not good—or can't be good—at math. Yet numbers and math, like letters and words, are simply a language we use to talk about the world.

I saw this dynamic play out with my daughter. Here was a kid I knew to be intelligent and clever, getting flustered and frustrated over math and perhaps even feeling like she was maybe not good enough. Fast forward, and she not only has proven to be an excellent entrepreneur but has also chosen careers that use math as a principal tool.

Just as your child will need basic reading skills, she will need arithmetic (basic math).

Use number toys. Read counting books. Encourage your child to count Cheerios on the table, how many stop signs you pass on the road, and how many cows are in the field.

Colors and Shapes

Learning colors and shapes teaches children terms for some of the ways we describe the world around us. Your child will also start to learn about sorting and classifying: all of these things are blue, some shapes and colors warn of danger. Recognizing shapes is also part of learning letters and numbers—which, after all, are just shapes too.

Music and Movement

Music and movement are fun. They help your child let off energy. And they help teach teamwork and expressiveness.

These multi-sensory experiences can enhance learning, too. For some children, songs and movement are a memory aid. How many of us learned our letters from the alphabet song? Or, used movement to help memorize things like the time's tables?

Ready for School

Help your youngster develop essential qualities to succeed in school: self-control, good manners, perseverance, and an eagerness to learn.

If your child has good manners and is well-behaved, he will make a good impression and you have already given him a step up on his first day of school. Teachers see a child who is polite and has self-control as a kid with a good attitude.

School isn't always easy. A child who has learned to try, and try again, will be ready to handle new academic tasks.

School will be a totally new experience for your child. So, no matter how nervous you might be too, be a cheerleader for this new experience. If you project enthusiasm, it will be easier for her to enter this new world.

SCHOOL

Once your kid enters school, you become less a teacher and more a coach.

Psychologist Madeline Levine (2020) talks about how we have made a transition from the concept of "nature or nurture," to "nature and nurture," and now to "nature with nurture." This is essentially the concept of nurturing the potential for excellence that is the nature of each individual—helping each child learn how to make the most of his capabilities.

This doesn't mean encouraging your child to believe she can do whatever she wants. It means encouraging her to master basic skills, pursue her interests, and be prepared for what may come.

Homework

Children today are given much more homework than there was before. When I was in school, homework didn't start until third grade and then it was less than half an hour a night. These days, that's how much homework some kindergarten students get.

Homework can be very stressful especially for kindergarten and beginning elementary students who need a lot of guidance with school work. Kids are tired when they get home from school. They need time to wind down and play. Parents are tired when they get home from work, too.

I recently saw a fascinating article from The Washington Post written by a parent who sent letters to her children's teachers to let them know that she was opting out of homework for her kindergarten and elementary school kids (Swanson, 2019).

It turns out this is something you can do. She reported that the teachers understood. One even said that she was assigning homework because some parents wanted it.

And the author's kids are doing well in school without the homework.

This strategy might be right for parents with kindergarten and young elementary-age students. As your child's parent/coach, what is your judgment for your kid?

But homework is valuable for older students. It teaches responsibility and time management. Homework that uses information taught in the classroom helps kids synthesize what they learn. So as your child's parent/coach, how can you help?

First, make sure your child has a good place to do homework. For younger kids, this is often the kitchen or dining room table where you can be nearby to help when needed.

Older kids may prefer to work in their room. Make sure they have a designated workplace that is well lit and comfortable. Help them establish a good homework routine. Remove distractions at homework time.

Perhaps your child would benefit from a study group. In elementary and middle school, my daughter and two of her friends used to come to our house after school every day and do homework together. They were able to help each other out, talk to each other about what they were learning, and sometimes teach each other if one of the kids was struggling. Teaching is a wonderful way to reinforce what you learn.

The three girls were able to finish their homework quickly and usually had time to play before dinner.

Remember parent/coach, you can advise and help revise, but don't DO your child's homework. It's your job to see that they do it. This means helping them figure out how much time their homework is going to take and when they need to start in order to get it done. If time is limited, it means helping them decide which is more important: working on an assignment that is due in two days or studying for the math test in the morning.

Tests

Tests are an unavoidable part of school: pop quizzes, unit tests, year-end exams, and standardized tests.

The only way to help prepare your kids for a pop quiz is to help them do their homework. Work with them on spelling words and math facts. Flashcards can be a very useful tool.

Anticipating tests makes some kids very anxious. There are a number of ways you can help:

- Make sure she gets enough sleep and has a good breakfast.
- Ask him what format the test will be. If he doesn't know, he can ask the teacher. It helps to know if you will be answering true/false, multiple-choice, or essay questions.
- Talk with your kid about what she has been learning. Explaining something to you will aid her recall and actually improve her understanding.
- Ask him what information he thinks will be on the test.
- If you know your child is a worrier, talk about things she can do to calm herself before the start of the test. Taking a couple of deep breaths can be very helpful.
- Tell him it's okay to skip over a question if he doesn't know the answer. It's better to move on in order to answer all the questions you do know.

If your child gets a disappointing grade on a test, don't be angry. Focus on how to do better.

Talk with him about study habits. Ask him about his routine. Does he think it would be best to do homework right away after school? Would it help to take 30 minutes to unwind after school before he starts his homework? Or, does he think it would be better to do his homework after dinner?

Ask her how she studied and what she thinks she should do differently the next time. Are there any distractions you can help her eliminate? Does she study at the same time every day? If not, suggest that she do so. Does she start with the easiest or the most difficult subject?

It's best to start with the tough things first when you have more energy for the job.

And be sure to mention the things they did well.

School Projects

If you are a parent who's been to a science fair, you've seen projects that you just know the kids could not have done by themselves. Doing things for your child may be satisfying for you but it doesn't let her learn anything. And, it teaches a bad lesson that there will always be someone who will do it for her.

On the other hand, teachers need to also consider projects that most children could accomplish by themselves, per their school grade. I'm often mystified by some of the projects children are asked to put together by themselves - surely they must know it's the parents who will end up doing it? I recently heard of a second-grade class that was asked to piece together a human skeleton using strips of paper, glue, and string - no other materials or variations allowed. On top of this, it was a next-day assignment. I'm sure many a parent started hyperventilating when they downloaded the homework that night.

Encourage your son to do things himself. Teach him how to ask for help. If he is struggling to come up with a project, help him choose something relevant, something that will help him learn, and that he can realistically do.

Often special projects in school are done in teams. Some parents are concerned that team members will bring their child down, but this misses the point. Teachers are well aware of who does what when students are working in teams.

At its best, project work teaches students how to collaborate. To work successfully together, children learn to be responsible. They learn how to disagree, how to listen, and how to respond to different points of view with substance not slogans.

Immaturity in public life today is very damaging to our children. It may be motivated by strategic political goals, but it flourishes when people do not know how to collaborate. Children need to learn that disagreement is not a threat.

The next time someone disagrees with you, notice how it makes you feel. You tense up, which can make you respond in a knee-jerk fashion instead of listening and then responding to the other point of view.

As a parent/coach, you can use dinner table conversations to teach and practice collaborative conversational skills.

Learning Disabilities

You are your child's best advocate.

If your child has trouble learning, it may be that they have a learning disability. The National Center for Learning Disabilities reports that 20% of children have some kind of learning disability (*The State of LD: Understanding the 1 in 5 - NCLD*, 2017).

Dyslexia affects the ability to read and spell. There are other specific issues related to numbers and math facts, writing and fine motor skills, interpretation of non-verbal cues, and oral or written comprehension. Attention Deficit Hyperactive Disorder (ADHD) is another problem that can affect a kid's ability to learn.

One sign that your child might have a learning disability is if he is still having tantrums and emotional meltdowns after four or five years of age. These are a sign of extreme frustration.

A learning disability can cause your child serious problems in school. Students with learning disabilities often have low self-esteem because they have trouble doing things that appear to come easily to their peers. Many of them end up repeating a grade, having discipline problems, and dropping out of school. More than half of young adults with a learning disability get involved with the legal system.

But, there are ways to cope with each type of learning disability.

Many people with learning disabilities are very successful. For example, organic chemistry is considered a difficult subject. I know an organic chemistry professor who has dyslexia, but he told me he became an organic chemist because it was easy for him. One of the abilities you need in that field is the ability to visualize in three dimensions. He could do that when most of his peers could not.

Or, you may have heard of Steven Spielberg, Michael Phelps, Tim Tebow, or Henry Winkler? All of these celebrities have one or more learning disabilities.

School shouldn't be hard at the kindergarten, first, or second-grade level. So if your kid tells you "I'm dumb," she's asking for help. Family history is significant, too, because learning disabilities tend to run in families.

If you suspect your child has a learning disability, get them tested so they can get help. Talk to the teacher. Some schools will push back about testing because they think the problem might be a developmental issue that will correct itself, but as a parent, you shouldn't accept that. If the school doesn't help, contact your pediatrician.

Tutoring is available through some schools or the school may be able to put you in touch with a free, subsidized, or low-cost tutoring service. You can get information online to contact one of the national learning disability associations if you need information or help.

It is best to act as soon as possible if your child is struggling with a learning disability because a lot of important foundational learning happens before age nine.

Special Needs

Other children who have health or physical limitations may need extra support to succeed in school. The Americans With Disabilities Act (ADA) requires schools to provide accommodations for these issues. The school will develop an Individual Education Program (IEP) for each child with special needs.

Schools have rules about how accommodations are provided. For example, even if your child has muscular dystrophy and is in a wheelchair, a school can't provide accommodations unless you have the proper paperwork to document the problem.

SPORTS AND OTHER EXTRACURRICULAR ACTIVITIES

According to the National Center for Education Statistics, students who participated in extracurricular activities had better attendance and got better grades (*Extracurricular Participation And Student Engagement*, 1995). Activities available to students outside the classroom include sports, music, performing arts, newspapers or yearbooks, academic clubs, vocational/professional clubs, service and hobby clubs, and student government.

These activities are also a great way for kids to meet other kids who share their interests.

Help your child get involved in activities that they will enjoy. If they try something one semester or one year and find they don't like it, it's okay to change. But encourage them to give the activity a real try.

STEER THEM AWAY FROM BEING PASSIVELY EDUCATED

Education is more than memorization. It is also learning how to think.

One of the most powerful ways to coach your kids is to say, "I don't know; let's find out." No one knows everything. Modeling how to handle learning things you don't know is an important life lesson. Your child will gain a lot of confidence if they have this ability because they will be able to educate themselves throughout life.

To handle our world of change, children need to be agile and creative, able to take advantage of opportunity when it presents itself. This often means learning new things.

Encourage your kids to think things through. Teach them the difference between a foolish risk and an educated risk. When you're talking about how to answer a question or solve a problem, guide them with the question, "And then what…?"

Rather than encourage your child to envision and prepare for a specific future, teach her how to prepare for twists and turns. When the future is uncertain, the one thing we do know is that change is likely. How your child reacts to change will have a big impact on his or her success.

Help your child cultivate creativity by encouraging him to explore his interests. Try not to judge. It's hard, for instance, if you see that your child excels in something, not to encourage her in that direction. You may think your child has what is needed to become a lawyer, a doctor, a teacher, or a salesperson. But what does she want? How can she use the talents you see in her to reach *her* dreams?

CHAPTER 7 PRAISE YOUR KIDS WHEN THEY DO WELL

PRAISE MAKES you feel good or at least it can. Praise makes you feel good if you think it is deserved and sincere.

How you use praise will have a big impact on your kids.

Praise isn't the same as love. Effective praise reminds kids of their value. This is why you should focus praise on their choices, actions, or effort.

PRAISE THINGS YOUR CHILD CAN CONTROL

How often have you heard someone say to a child, "You're so pretty" or "That's so smart?" There's no need to tell your daughter she's pretty or your son he's smart—the world will tell them that.

The most powerful way to praise your child is to focus on things your child can control.

Rather than saying, "You look pretty," say "You chose a nice outfit for school today." Being pretty is an accident of nature so being praised for that may feel undeserved. But being praised for putting together a good outfit for school is an aspect of appearance that your daughter can control.

Instead of saying to your son, "You're so smart" or "What great grades," say "I know you worked hard and deserve these grades." If you praise the results instead of the process, he may feel that he's loved for the grades. Then if he gets a bad grade, he might feel anxious about your love.

Research done at Stanford University in 1998 bears this out (Underwood, 2020). The study compared the impact of praising children who were successful in doing a task by telling them that they were smart, compared to another group of children who were successful and praised for their hard work.

Children who were praised for their hard work were more willing to choose to work on more challenging problems because they were confident about their abilities. Children who were praised for being smart tended to avoid more challenging problems for fear of failure.

Your child will focus on what you praise.

SHOW EXCITEMENT FOR THEIR ACHIEVEMENTS, BUT ALSO PAY ATTENTION SO YOU CAN BE SPECIFIC

It's okay to sometimes praise your child by saying "I know you worked hard." It is better, however, to pay attention to what your child is doing so that you can be specific with your praise.

Specific praise makes it clear to your child that you are paying attention.

If your daughter shows you the block tower she built, you might praise her choice of blocks or how careful she was. If your son shows you a painting he's done, praise his color selection or combination of paints and stickers, in addition to the end result.

Use praise to encourage your child's engagement with what she does. If you see that your daughter worked hard and enthusiastically on a science fair project, you might comment "I saw how much you enjoyed working on this."

And avoid praising your child by comparing him to someone else. This creates competition where there need not be any, and it focuses your child's attention on how he's doing in relation to his peers rather than in relation to his own capabilities.

EMPATHIZE WHEN THEY DON'T DO WELL

If your child makes a mistake and admits it, praise them for telling the truth, and ask what they can do differently in the future.

If your daughter has not done well at school or not behaved well on a playdate, talk with her privately. You don't want to shame or embarrass your kid.

It is okay to criticize behavior. You want to correct bad behavior. But don't criticize the person. For instance, imagine your young child is at the playground and shouts to one of her friends, "No. You can't play!" You can tell her, "That sounded very rude." Don't say, "You are rude."

Balance criticism with recognition of what your child did right in the situation. Research shows that praising what went right instead of criticizing what went wrong is a more powerful strategy for improving results (Dewar, 2019b).

DON'T OVERDO IT

Too much praise can be damaging. The child may see overdone praise as something undeserved that they can't live up to. Or, if praise seems too good to be true, the child may push the limits to see what will happen.

Children need to value themselves. As a parent, this means walking that fine line between praise and criticism.

If you give too much praise, the child may feel the praise is not warranted and that they don't or can't meet the standard you expect. If you give too little praise, the child may not recognize when they are doing well.

A similar balance is important with criticism, too. If you give too much criticism, your son may feel like he is being attacked or come to believe that he is bad. Too little criticism and your daughter won't recognize when what she is doing is wrong.

Children always need your support and often that support comes in the form of praise. But use it wisely. Too much praise can be demotivating or even damaging.

WHO IS BEING PRAISED?

I have met parents who are in constant competition with their own kids; they deny them praise or use backhanded praise in order to make everything about themselves. I'm talking about narcissism.

If you're around a narcissistic parent you might hear something like, "He's just like me. He's going to be in the NBA". These are parents you may hear screaming to their kid about what to do from the sidelines during a Pee-Wee league soccer game.

A narcissistic parent is one who lives through or feels themselves to be in competition with their child. This might be a mother who wants to be the most beautiful one in the family or a father who wishes he could have been a professional basketball player and sees that potential in his son. The result is a child who is not loved for being himself but is loved for meeting the parent's expectations.

We all want the best for our children. Sometimes it can be hard to resist the thought that what you wanted for yourself is also best for your child, without regard to what he wants for himself. Wanting the best for your child is not narcissistic. But ask yourself, how do you define what is best? What is best for your child should be based on your child's interests and abilities, not your dreams.

Unfortunately, children of narcissistic parents are likely to grow into fragile adults, with low self-esteem and limited ability to deal independently with life's ups and downs. To avoid raising a narcissistic child, focus your praise on what he does rather than who he is. Be realistic about your child's accomplishments. When she has done well, tell her that she worked very hard, not that she's very smart or special.

THE POWER OF PRAISE WHEN THINGS GO WRONG

This may seem counterintuitive, but I've also found that praise is a powerful tool to use at the end of a rough day.

Praise to a child is like watering a plant. It nourishes the behaviors that you want.

Imagine. It has been a long day. In the morning, your daughter didn't want to get out of bed and you ended up running late. In the evening, she got into a fight with her brother about what they were going to watch on TV and then she pitched a fit about going to bed. You're tired. You just want her to go to sleep so you can have some time yourself to decompress.

But—instead of rushing through bedtime or talking with your daughter about some of her bad behavior and asking her not to do that again—try talking with your daughter about what went well.

Tell her, "I noticed today how you had your backpack ready before school. And you did a nice job clearing the table tonight. Thank you. Now, it's been a long day, and you need your sleep. Good night. I love you." You might also ask her, "Tell me something good about your day."

Try it! This really works.

Think of it as a gratitude journal. Praising your daughter for things she did well on a rough day shows her that you were paying attention. It reminds her that you think she is a good person. And it focuses her attention on good behavior. This is particularly powerful at the end of the day, right before sleep, because sleep is when memories are made.

CHAPTER 8
HELP THEM BE COMFORTABLE WITH BEING THEMSELVES

THERE ARE lots of things involved in defining who we are. Some are matters of choice: our work, religion, and politics. Others are intrinsic: like gender, race, and ethnicity.

As children grow, they ask themselves: Who am I? How do I fit in my family and in the world? Answering these questions of identity is part of growing up.

WHAT TO DO WHEN YOUR CHILD IS STRUGGLING

Appearance

Children become aware of their appearance at a very young age. It's one of the first things children hear (What an adorable baby! She's so beautiful! What a handsome boy!). I suppose people say these things because there's not much else to comment on about an infant!

Then, as children are exposed to the media, they start to learn false notions of what people really look like. Airbrushed, photoshopped images are not real, but kids don't know that. And so they pursue a false idea of what they should look like.

Body image problems can result. Children come to believe that they must have a perfect body and that having a perfect body will make them happy. This is most often a problem for girls, but boys can have body image issues, too.

A young girl who develops early or who is not skinny like her friends may start to think of herself as fat. Girls with body image problems can develop eating disorders like anorexia or bulimia. These are life-threatening.

A young boy who is not developing as quickly as some of the other boys in his class may start to think of himself as a weakling. Boys with body image problems more often suffer from depression.

Parents have a large role to play to help their kids develop a healthy body image:

- Model what it means to think in a healthy way about your body.
- Talk about healthy eating, not dieting.
- Help your kids develop healthy eating habits.
- Serve a good variety of healthy food.
- Serve right-sized portions. Your kids need to know what a reasonable portion actually is. For example, the McDonald's kid's meal used to be their standard meal for adults. Now the standard adult meal is a quarter pounder that is three times that size. And drinks come in quart-sized tubs.
- Don't tell your kids they must always clean their plate. Tell them, instead, to eat slowly and stop when they are full.
- Talk about exercising to build strength, not to lose weight.
- Talk about being a good person, not about looking good.

Pay attention when you hear your son or daughter talking about their body. Don't ignore it if you hear your daughter say her thighs are too big. Ask her why she thinks so. Talk about being healthy and how everyone is different.

Comment when you see things in the media that aren't real or if you see someone who may look nice but is behaving badly.

It's normal for adolescents to be hyper-aware of their bodies. Empathize with the changes your adolescent is experiencing, but make sure that body image issues aren't leading to depression or an eating disorder.

Social media is a particular problem today. One recent example is the impact of Instagram on teenagers' body image.

According to the Wall Street Journal, the unrealistically 'perfect' images teenage girls see on Instagram are tied directly to teen suicide (Wallace, 2021). Instagram's own researchers have found that six percent of American teenage users trace a desire to kill themselves to Instagram. Thirty percent of teenage girls and fourteen percent of teenage boys say that Instagram makes them feel worse about themselves.

Be aware of the danger signs:

- Children who are depressed may lack energy, pull back from friends and activities, have more trouble controlling their emotions, change their sleep and / or eating patterns, and spend lots more time alone.
- Children with an eating disorder will show an excessive weight change and you will notice new eating patterns. They may eat too little or start skipping meals, or eat too much and disappear into the bathroom right after eating.

Call the doctor if you suspect your child has health issues related to body image.

Special Needs

If you are a parent whose child has special needs, you are on what the Center for Parent Information and Resources calls "the unplanned journey." This is not what you imagined when you learned you were going to have a child.

Parenting a child who has special needs can expand your heart in ways you never imagined. But, it is also challenging and emotionally draining. It puts extra stress on the family and requires more from you.

At times you may feel uncertain, angry, frustrated, or sad. You may envy parents whose children are 'normal,' and feel guilty about how you feel. Don't. It's natural.

Acknowledge how you feel.

Every parent is advised to enjoy the little things. This can be much more meaningful now.

Join a support group. Arm yourself with as much information as you can find about resources and services.

Make time for yourself every day, even if it's only five minutes before you get up in the morning. Do things that are just for you—coffee with a friend, a manicure, or a date night. Remember, you need to take care of yourself in order to take care of your child.

Do not isolate yourself or your child. Family and friends can be a great source of support. It's okay to ask for and accept their help.

Food Allergies

In 2008, the CDC's National Center for Health Statistics reported that nearly four percent of children in the U.S. had a food allergy. By 2020 that number had doubled to eight percent. In a typical American classroom today, there are likely to be two children with food allergies.

The discovery of a food allergy comes as a terrible shock for the parent who must rush their baby to the emergency room with a life-threatening reaction to his first taste of egg. It is devastating for a family when their teenager, who knew he was allergic to peanuts, dies because he thought it would be okay to try just one pistachio.

There is no cure for food allergies, so parents need to make sure their kids avoid—always avoid—the food allergen.

If your kid has a food allergy you will need to be prepared for emergencies, such as having an epi-pen on hand. Playdates, starting school, travel—all of these things will cause anxiety.

It is crucial to educate your child, who must handle his allergy for life. Also educate other family members, teachers and school staff, and family friends to help protect your child.

Organizations like Food Allergy Research & Education (FARE), Kids With Food Allergies (KFA), and other advocacy groups are there to provide resources and support.

Developmental, Behavioral, Physical, or Mental Issues

They are rare, but there is a constellation of other serious challenges a child and parent might face. These range from potentially correctable conditions like birth defects or childhood cancer, to chronic issues like Down syndrome, sickle cell anemia, diabetes, or muscular dystrophy.

These diagnoses are overwhelming. Every child, and every situation, is unique. But know that there are others, dealing with similar problems, who will understand.

As with food allergies, there are dedicated advocacy organizations and support groups you can turn to for help.

Identity

Identity issues are complicated, emotionally charged, and often misunderstood.

Parents of children who struggle with identity issues have to deal with the situation for themselves as well as helping their child.

Many parents tie up part of their own identity in their child. How often do you hear about the football dad who lives through his athlete son? Or the mom who, perhaps unconsciously, guides her daughter to the future she would have liked.

Know that identity issues are not a matter of choice. They simply are. It's no one's fault. You are not to blame. Your job is to love and support your child.

To provide support it is important for you to be open, ask questions, and listen to what your child has to say.

Sexual Identity

Being lesbian, gay, bisexual, or transgender is no longer as stigmatizing as it was when I was a child. But, the stigmas are still out there and the challenges are real.

Many LGBT children report that coming out to their parents was the most difficult thing they had to do because, when they came out, they feared losing their parents' love and support.

It's complicated. I know of one teacher whose students nominated him as the person they were most likely to approach if they were struggling with their sexual identity. Yet this teacher's own son felt his dad would be devastated if his son was gay.

If your child comes out to you, let her know she is loved. Be open to what she has to say. Make sure she knows you will always be there. Ask questions and keep an open dialogue. Help her navigate dating in a safe, appropriate way.

Gender Identity

While being gay, lesbian, or bisexual is about who you think is sexually attractive, being transgender is about whether who you are on the inside matches how you look on the outside.

Gender identity may seem to be a new issue, but it is not. Cross-dressing has been around for centuries. What is new is the ability to change gender identity medically.

The first sex change operation on record was in 1930. A Danish painter who was born male was reassigned female. The surgery was highly experimental and she died in 1931. In 1952, American Christine Jorgensen transitioned from male to female and became a famous advocate for transgender people. Today, even some young children are given sex-changing treatment.

There is controversy about what it means for a child to question his gender identity before puberty and how early it is appropriate to address gender reassignment.

Lots of girls are tomboys. There are boys who play dress-up in women's clothes. This is not the same as believing your physical gender is wrong. A sex-change operation is irreversible and not to be taken lightly. So if you are concerned, how do you know if your child has real gender identity issues? Some key signs include:

- Insisting they are the other gender,
- Strongly preferring cross-gender roles during play and dressing in clothes of the opposite gender, and
- Expressing hate for their own sexual anatomy.

There are serious physical and mental issues to address if your child is transgender. Treatment involves working for years with a team of professionals as you figure out how best to proceed.

Adoption

All children who are adopted will at some point wonder about their biological identity, and they may have little or no information available to them. Children who are adopted into a family of a different race can have additional identity issues.

Other children can be naively cruel asking, "Why don't you look like your parents?" or saying, "Your mother isn't your real mommy." Help your children learn how to respond to these kinds of taunts.

As an adoptive parent, don't brush your child's identity questions aside. Be open about the fact that he is adopted, that he is wanted, and that you love everything about him.

It is natural for young children to define identity superficially: people who look like me. Part of growing up involves expanding your identity to include such invisible qualities as people who act or think like me. Be proactive to recognize and affirm the qualities you and your adopted child share. Recognize and respect the differences.

Answer her questions. Help her figure out how she wants to answer questions that her friends and peers will ask.

If it is a trans-racial adoption, help them learn everything they can about that part of their identity.

Understand and be supportive if, as she grows up, your daughter wants to learn as much as possible about her biological parents. Or, your son wants to meet his birth mother. Their biological parents are a part of the child you love. Welcome their being open with you.

BULLYING

Bullying is often a problem for children with special needs, but the problem of bullying is much more pervasive than that.

Bullying is on the rise. It affects children in life, primarily in school, and increasingly in the digital realm. Teasing, name-calling, and rough-housing happen with children. But these things can escalate and become bullying.

Bullying is unwanted aggressive behavior from one child against another. It can be physical aggression, verbal harassment, social exclusion, or cyber-bullying. Cyberbullying takes the problem out of school and into the home. It can be anonymous. And it can go viral. In 2018, the CDC reported that around 15% of high school students reported being involved in cyber-bullying.

Look for these signs to warn that your child might be bullied:

- Your child comes home with missing or damaged things
- She starts taking a different way home from school
- He often complains that he doesn't feel well

- She is depressed or has trouble sleeping
- He begins to do badly in school
- She is upset after spending time on the computer or her phone

These things aren't always a sign of bullying, but if your child has one or more of these problems, you should try to find out if bullying is the cause. Don't wait. Deal with the problem right away.

If the bullying is happening at school:

- Encourage your child to stand up to the bully.
- Teach your child coping skills.
- Encourage your child not to engage with a cyberbully.
- Contact the bully's parents if you know who it is and the problem persists.
- If the bullying escalates, document what is happening and talk to the teacher or principal to report what's going on and enlist their help to stop it.

THE PRINCIPLE OF FULL ACCEPTANCE

One of the ways that people make sense of the world is to categorize things. In doing so, we categorize other people based on our perception of such things as their sex, race, age, social status, or job.

Unfortunately, this tendency can lead to stereotyping, prejudice and discrimination. Often these biases are unconscious. For example, if you are talking to your son about his sexuality and say something like, "Some of my best friends are gay," you are revealing hidden bias. In this case, you have a stereotypical mental image of what it means to be gay but you are saying that your friends don't fit that image.

There was an experiment—famous to psychologists—where people were asked to group insects and flowers into categories. The study showed that it was much easier for people to put flowers into categories with pleasant names and insects into categories with unpleasant names.

This has implications for parents who are dealing with their child's identity issues because, no matter how we see ourselves, we all categorize. We all have mental stereotypes and hidden biases.

So when you are talking with your child, be very aware of how he or she reacts to what you say. They will be very attuned to any hidden bias.

Be honest if you perceive that something you say strikes your child the wrong way. Acknowledge it. Apologize. And always remind your child of your love and support.

CHAPTER 9 NEVER LET YOUR CHILD GO TO SLEEP UPSET

CHILDREN LEARN by testing their limits, so conflict is inevitable. Children also have a harder time controlling themselves when they are tired, so they will often have outbursts at the end of the day.

One of the more important—and challenging—things you can do as a parent is to help your child get a good night's sleep by making sure he doesn't go to sleep upset.

This is backed up by research into sleep (Andrews 2010). We know that two things happen during healthy sleep. Your brain "cleans house," restoring cells and getting rid of toxins that built up during the day. Your brain also consolidates and processes the information you learned during the day, creating memories you won't forget.

So healthy sleep is very important. But being upset causes stress and stress interrupts healthy sleep.

Stress-free sleep enables the body, mind, and emotions to recharge, getting you ready to face the coming day. This is true for your kids —and you.

DEALING WITH EXPLOSIVE OUTBURSTS, TANTRUMS, AND OTHER MISBEHAVIOR

Keep Your Own Anger and Frustration in Check

I remember a joke a friend once told me: If your young child is misbehaving and you feel like you are losing control, take his milk bottle and fill it up with half gin and half Vodka, and drink it yourself. Everything will become a memory. If only it were true!

With a child you can't mask the problem, you have to deal with it right away. When emotions are riding high, it's more important than ever for you to get yourself under control. This means you need to deal with yourself before you deal with your child.

When confronted with a kid's tantrum or misbehavior, your own emotions are at the surface, too. This is heightened by the fact that you are dealing with one of the people who matters more to you than anyone in the world.

Consider the source. This is what my mother told me once when a bully at school was making me feel bad. She told me that the bully was being mean because he was unhappy with himself. Her advice helped me let the bully's words roll off my back. I've found it to be good advice to use when dealing with my kids, too.

You're an adult. They're kids. They're learning, and they are learning from you.

The little person who just pushed your buttons is still learning what emotions are. Outbursts happen before he knows how to communicate about and control them.

The teenager who has just pushed your buttons is living in a flood of hormones and coping with a host of new emotional challenges in her life. Sometimes, things just boil over for her.

So, take a deep breath. Mentally, tell yourself to calm down. Visualize the behavior you want—from yourself and your child.

Mastering emotions is an important lesson you teach by example.

No one is perfect. There will be times when your anger and frustration will show. What's important is to try not to let your own emotions determine how you react to your child.

On the occasions when you do react with exasperation or anger, as long as your child is safe, it's okay to walk away for a moment. Collect yourself. Apologize to your kid then deal with the problem.

Your kid will benefit from knowing that you, too, have strong emotions and that you know how to control them.

Discipline the Behavior, Not the Emotion

I read a lot of online blogs about parenting, and I recently saw a story about a dad who lost control with his 3-year-old son who wouldn't go to bed.

It was before bedtime. The dad had been teaching his son not to hit, but the son got angry and punched his dad in the leg. The dad got angry, picked up the boy, and rushed through their nighttime routine. Turning out the lights, the dad started to close the door, without telling his son "I love you" the way he usually did.

But just as the dad was leaving the room, he heard a small whisper. He went back in to ask his son what he had said. And the son quietly repeated his part of the routine, "I love you, Dad."

The dad went back into the room and cuddled his son. He told him that he loved him, too, and that he was a good boy even though hitting is a bad thing to do.

This dad had established a strong, loving bedtime routine with his son. The son held on to that routine to help himself feel better, which helped the dad as well.

In the end, the dad and the son were both able to let go of their anger before they went to sleep.

Having a consistent nighttime routine creates a strong basis for helping you to make sure your child does not go to sleep upset.

Tantrums are natural. They start when your child realizes she has the power to say yes or no, to decide how she will behave. A tantrum is often triggered when you say 'no' to something your child wants. You need to remember that this reaction is because she doesn't know how to handle what she thinks and feels.

Perhaps your child is angry because he wants you to read another story. Your routine is to read two stories before bed. Now he wants one more.

You say 'No' because that's your routine. He's angry because he can't get his way. What can you do to calm the storm? Discipline the behavior, not the emotion.

- Stay calm. Don't yell.
- Help your son name what he's feeling: "I know you are mad, but you know we just read two stories before bed." Or for an

older child you might say, "Use your words and tell me what's wrong."

- Give him time to get over his anger and calm down. Stay close. Be there for him, but don't change your mind.
- If your son doesn't calm down, try to distract him: "Would you like me to give you a hug?"
- When your son has quieted down, praise him: "Good job calming down. I love you."

Bring On the Happy

For parents, a goal when their kids have tantrums is to help them learn how to calm down—how to self-regulate.

If he cries, don't try to stop him. Hold him and let him cry it out. Tears release stress from our body. When a toddler has a tantrum, he is overwhelmed with feeling—totally stressed. When he cries, he releases his stress.

Try not to communicate to your kid that the feelings that caused the tantrum are bad. Everyone has feelings of anger, frustration, or fear. We need to learn to acknowledge and get control of them.

Once your child has let it out, she is ready to calm down and listen to you. Empathize with your child's feelings. Show that you accept what she feels, even if you don't agree with it. If she feels understood, it will be easier for her to move on.

Then, to bring on the happy. Give your child some positive attention.

You might show him how you use deep breaths to calm down—you could even try playing "in with the good air, out with the bad".

Praise her for being ready to go to sleep. Give her a hug. Tell her you love her.

EXPRESS YOUR LOVE

We have so many ways to say "I love you" to our kids!

The words are important. Use them.

Act lovingly. Back your words up with actions.

I'm not talking about giving material gifts or rewards. Giving a gift as a reward for good behavior sends a bad message. It will teach your kid to be manipulative and materialistic. As someone once told me, "The reward for doing good is doing good."

Using a gift to reward good behavior is a bribe. It will teach her she can get what she wants by acting out. It will teach him to bargain with you to get what he wants rather than simply behave as he should because it is the right thing to do.

A classic example of bribery in action is the harassed mom with a toddler in the shopping cart: "Be quiet and I'll let you have those cookies" she says. Her kid is going to be quiet for the moment, but this story doesn't end well. What the kid is learning is: "I don't need to be quiet and behave in the store. If I pitch a fit, Mom will get me what I want."

So, express your love through discipline—through making what is expected of your kids clear. Let them know that you believe they can understand and do the right thing.

Saying 'no' is actually one of the ways you express love because 'no' sets clear boundaries. Boundaries let kids know what you expect and how they should behave.

We also express our love by sticking with our kid through the emotional storm. She is showing the love and trust she has for you by feeling free to express what she feels. Reciprocate by being there for her. Teach her better ways to respond.

Use touch and loving glances.

No matter what has happened during the day, or how tempestuous it is at bedtime, a parent can create the appropriate environment for their child to go to bed happy—bad mood resolved.

TALK IT OUT

When kids are upset, there's a reason. Understanding why your kid is acting out will help you help them.

I have a game that I have played with all my kids. I used to call it "Daddy's Pow-Wow," but lately, I started to call it "Time Out with Daddy." If there was a problem, we would lay together on the floor and, even if we were mad at each other, we would hug and kiss, and we would talk out the problem.

I try not to talk too much initially and let my kid do most of the talking. That is the only way to find out why they were acting up. Once I know the problem, I can try to help them find a solution. You won't always solve things 100%, but the most important thing you can do is not judge.

An advantage I have today with my youngest compared to when my older children were little is that I studied Conflict Mediation about ten years ago at the University of Nevada, Las Vegas. I learned that instead of having to mediate two sides of a conflict, you have only one side to mediate (in my case, my son's). The language of mediation helps me ask questions that are not upsetting. I ask questions that will help my son understand and resolve his issues. With children, this is really good because it lets us communicate in adult terms without forgetting that they are children.

ACCEPTANCE VS FORGIVENESS

Kids make mistakes. That's how they learn.

When they misbehave, what's the point of getting angry, yelling at them, and demanding an apology? I believe it better serves your child —and you—if you practice acceptance rather than forgiveness.

Accept that your kid misbehaved. Explain why her behavior was wrong or misguided. Let her recognize and understand her own accountability.

Acceptance means that you know that kids will mess up. It means accepting that the child you love has something to learn and taking the steps to teach her. This attitude is the best mindset for a parent when dealing with a child's transgressions.

Don't create a situation where your child feels like he needs to earn forgiveness. An attitude of forgiveness can be damaging because it can end up being used by parents as a judgmental tool.

Forgiveness usually involves feelings of shame. It is not a good strategy when you are disciplining—teaching—your child because shame is personal. It focuses on who the child is rather than how the child has behaved. As a result, kids are led to feel shame ("I am bad") rather than guilt ("What I did was bad").

If you take an attitude of forgiveness, your kid might be defiant because he feels that, since he is bad, there's nothing he can do to correct his behavior. Or your daughter may be defiant because she thinks the judgment is unjust.

Acceptance focuses on the behavior rather than the child. It helps your child learn from her mistakes. Forgiveness causes stress.

WAYS TO ALLEVIATE STRESS

What's wrong with stress?

Stress is a survival mechanism. It's how the body responds to danger. Your heart beats faster, your blood pressure goes up, you breathe more quickly, and your body releases stress hormones. In the face of a more serious threat, you tense up, perhaps even sweat. Your body is ready for action.

This is natural, but too much stress is poison.

We call stress the fight or flight response. It is a big help when you need to fight off a saber-tooth tiger, run up a hill, or get out of the way of a moving car. It can be too much, however, in the modern world where danger and perceived threats are usually not life-threatening.

Chronic, low-level stress causes toxins to build up in the mind and body. In children, chronic stress interferes with healthy growth. Children who grow up with chronic stress are more likely to have developmental delays. They are more likely to have issues with substance abuse or depression and suffer from chronic health problems like diabetes or heart disease.

As a parent, you want to provide a supportive environment for your child to learn to cope with the stresses of everyday life. You also want to limit your child's exposure to very stressful situations.

Sometimes that's simply not possible. Poverty, natural disasters, or bullying are all causes of extreme stress. But it has been shown that a loving, supportive relationship can buffer your child from the worst effects of extreme stress.

At the start of this chapter, I talked about how the brain "cleans house" and reinforces memories while we are asleep. That's what happens during healthy, natural sleep. Stress interferes with this process.

This is why not letting your child go to sleep upset is at the core of my personal learning as a parent. Life is too short, and it is simply not worth it for your child—or you—to go to sleep upset.

You should always be calm before you go to sleep, and it is important to reach this state naturally without Xanax or happy pills. Pharmaceuticals interfere with natural sleep.

We know that there is a strong connection between our bodies and our minds. Now the science of neuroplasticity is revealing more and more about our brain's amazing power to affect our body.

What we are learning from neuroplasticity is that, if something is wrong, we can stimulate the brain to rewire itself to help fix the problem. In extreme cases, something that was being handled in one part of the brain can even be transferred to a different part of the brain. This is how a person who has lost the ability to speak due to a brain injury can re-learn how to talk.

If the brain can do that, we most certainly have the power to rewire our thoughts and emotions in response to stress.

This is why I feel so strongly about the importance of teaching children how to alleviate stress. Here are some good techniques I have found. They are useful for life, not just after a temper tantrum.

Parent-Child Meditations

Meditation strengthens the mind. Through meditation, you can increase attention and focus, as well as the ability to regulate emotion. You can reduce anxiety, depression, anger, and fear.

There is evidence that links meditation to improved brain function and research that shows meditation can improve the body's ability to heal. Some of the most persuasive of this research has been done by University of Wisconsin neuroscientist, Richard Davidson together with the Dalai Lama (A look into the science of well-being and the Healthy Minds Framework from the Center for Healthy Minds at UW–Madison - Center for Healthy Minds, n.d.).

Meditation has helped me become more aware and less judgmental. I feel it has made me a better parent. And I meditate together with my son.

We use an app called Headspace, which has separate apps for parents and kids, as well as focused meditations for scores of different purposes, including happiness, self-esteem, anger, stress, or sports.

Yoga and Other Stretching Exercises

Yoga is an ancient Indian discipline whose purpose is to bring harmony to body and mind. Yoga enhances flexibility, balance and coordination, and promotes relaxation. There are many different types of yoga. My son and I have taken Hatha Yoga classes, and he tells me that it makes him feel good. Classes are important so you can make sure you do the poses correctly.

There is a lot of evidence for the benefits of yoga. Johns Hopkins Medicine lists 9 benefits, including managing stress, brightening your mood, and helping you sleep better (*9 Benefits of Yoga*, n.d.). A Harvard University blog cites evidence that yoga improves mental and physical health for children, including reducing anxiety and stress (Wei, 2016). The site offers suggestions for simple yoga exercises and games kids will enjoy.

Homeopathy and Naturopathy

Homeopathy is a system that was developed in Germany in the late 1700s. Homeopathic remedies are administered in minimal doses. Treatment starts with a long 1-2 hour consultation. This type of consultation alone can be very beneficial at a time when you are lucky to get ten minutes with your regular doctor. Sometimes it's important simply to be heard.

Naturopathy is a similar, but distinct, type of health practice. It uses some homeopathic remedies, as well as herbal medicine, nutrition, lifestyle, hydrotherapy, natural supplements, bodywork, and counseling.

There is little research evidence of the effectiveness of these practices. But both are becoming more popular in the U.S., and many patients report therapeutic results.

Energy Healing

Energy healing is a form of alternative medicine that is based on the idea of balancing the energy that flows through the human body.

Balancing this energy promotes well-being and reduces anxiety and stress. There are many techniques:

- Reiki and Healing Touch—These techniques involve placing the hands above energy points in the body.
- Reconnective Healing—This healing approach is simple enough that kids can learn how to use it too.
- QiGong and Tai Chi—These are both ancient Chinese wellness practices that promote health through meditation, gentle movement, and controlled breathing.
- Acupuncture—This ancient Chinese therapy uses very thin needles that are inserted at points of the body related to the flow of energy, or Qi. There is clinical evidence that acupuncture is an effective treatment for a variety of physical and emotional issues.
- Massage and Reflexology—When you get a massage, the therapist rubs and kneads your body to relieve pain and tension. Once the province of expensive spas, massage is now offered in hospitals and clinics and is even available in retail outlets in airports and shopping malls. Reflexology is a special type of massage that involves applying pressure just to specific points on the feet or hands. Reflexology is a proven therapy to reduce anxiety and stress.

I know that some of the techniques listed here may be considered controversial, especially when they are promoted as an alternative to modern medicine. There is little to no clinical evidence to support their ability to cure disease. But there is a lot of anecdotal evidence of their efficacy from patients who are enthusiastic about the results.

My interest in all of these techniques is focused on their ability to reduce stress. This is proven.

Stress can make you sick. My family and I have tried and benefited from the stress-relieving capacity of them all.

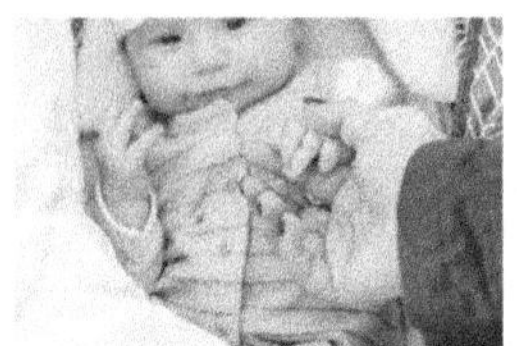

CHAPTER 10
ALWAYS REMEMBER YOU ARE THE PARENT

YOUR CHILD NEEDS you as a parent, not as a friend.

There will be time to develop deep friendships once your child no longer depends on the structure and mentoring you provide. In fact, being able to be a friend to your adult child is one of the greatest joys of parenthood.

But that comes later.

At the beginning of this book, I quoted Dr. T. Berry Brazelton who says, "Discipline is teaching, not punishment." But that's not the complete thought. In the preceding paragraph, Brazelton writes (2015):

Discipline is the second most important gift that a parent provides for a child. Of course, love is the first. But the safety that a child finds in discipline is essential, for without discipline, there are no boundaries. Children need boundaries and find comfort in them. They know they are loved when a parent cares enough to give the gift of discipline. (p. xxi)

YOU ARE IN CHARGE

As the parent, you are in charge. That is your function in the family when your children are growing up.

This role may seem clearer when your children are infants. It's obvious that infants need you to do everything: feed them, bathe them, diaper and change them, and protect them from harm.

As they get older, children still need food, clothing, shelter, and protection. They also need discipline—guidance for how to behave. They need you to establish rules, to let them push back against the rules, and to know that you will require them to follow the rules. They need to know that you expect good behavior and that you know they can deliver it.

But in fact, even infants need love with discipline.

For example, babies communicate by crying. A new parent soon notices that different cries mean different things. There's the cry that says "I'm awake, where are you?" The ones that say: "I'm hungry," "I'm wet," "I don't feel good," or "I'm bored."

Once you know the different ways your infant fusses and cries, you will need to decide when and how to respond. "I don't feel good" needs your attention right away. But if you pick your baby up for a cuddle at the first whimper of "I'm bored," you can stunt his ability to solve problems for himself. As long as he's okay, your infant needs to be able to soothe himself when he cries.

Parents with more than one child usually find that the second, third or fourth child learns this lesson well, because they often have to wait for attention until Mommy takes care of everyone else!

Your kids actually want you to be in charge. You have experience. You understand the things that make them feel confused and anxious. Knowing you are in charge makes them feel secure.

DON'T BE AFRAID THEY WILL HATE YOU

Some parents fall into the trap of wanting so much for their child to like them, they try to be their child's friend.

You are not your child's friend. Friends are peers, they're equals. But you are in control. And—even though it may not seem that way—that's how your child wants it to be.

Being a parent, providing rules, and enforcing them can be tough because it means you have to tell your child, 'No.' A parent's love means providing guidance and support based on what your child needs not what your child wants.

As a result, you will probably hear your toddler shout, "You're mean, Daddy. I hate you!" You're likely to hear the h-word from young children, preteens, and even teenagers, too.

But remember—'hate' doesn't mean the same thing to a kid that it means to an adult. When a kid uses the word 'hate,' she isn't really talking about you. She is trying to express her frustration or anger.

It's hard, but don't take it personally.

When your toddler says "I hate you," she is just learning what words mean. Try not to react. If she sees you react, she's going to use the word over and over again.

An older child does know what the word 'hate' means. When he uses it, he's likely angry, and he is trying to hurt you. Don't react and don't engage. In fact, your best response may be, "I'm sorry because I love you."

At first, your child probably doesn't know how else to communicate what he feels. If he keeps on using the h-word, start talking with him about what he is feeling and how being told "I hate you" makes you feel.

With a younger child, the reason behind what he feels is likely to be clearly apparent to you.

When your pre-teen or teenage daughter shouts "I hate you," she also knows what she is saying. But chances are, the problem that she's wrestling with is more complex. You will have to talk with her to find out what's going on. Listen to everything she says so you have an idea of what is bothering her. Then when she has calmed down, you can talk things through.

Young children don't understand the effect their words can have—that's part of what they need you to teach them.

Also, take the opportunity to talk with your child about better ways to act when they are upset. Teach your child that, just like they shouldn't hit someone else, they shouldn't use words to hurt someone else.

PARENTING IS NOT A SHOW OF FORCE OR HOW TO USE "BECAUSE I SAY SO"

How many times have you heard a parent say to a child in exasperation, "Do it because I say so!"? How many times have you said this yourself?

We parents all do!

"Because I say so" is a show of force. In some situations, it's the only thing you can say. But it shouldn't be a place to start.

Parents need to use force to keep their toddlers safe. When your toddler is reaching for that sharp knife, do you really want to reason with him? Of course not. You stop him. Only then can you explain, "I don't want you to cut yourself. That knife is sharp."

As your child gets older and you say "Don't touch that," she will start to ask, "Why?" At this point using "Because I say so" is controlling. It's a show of force when what your daughter needs is to learn what your rules are and why they matter. When she understands the rules, she can decide to follow them when you're not around.

If your daughter is reaching for a piece of paper you've laid on the table and you say "Don't touch that," you probably aren't protecting her from harm. You're likely to be protecting your work from getting messed up. You have time to say, "Please don't touch that."

When she asks "Why?" you can explain, "Because I need it later." Your daughter will start to learn that one of the rules is "don't touch everything you see."

But what if she reaches for the paper again? You say, "I asked you not to touch that." What if she replies, "I want to draw a picture. Why can't I have it?"

You calmly say, "I just told you why."

If she comes back with, "That's not fair. I want to draw a picture now," then "Because I say so" is okay.

You gave direction. You explained your reason. Now you are enforcing the rule.

GIVE LOVE UNCONDITIONALLY, EARN THEIR RESPECT

What Is Unconditional Love?

We've talked a little about unconditional love.

I experienced this love from my parents. Then I came to understand it much more deeply at the first glimpse of my first child. It was a punch in the gut. I knew right away I would do anything for him. And I feel that way about all of my children.

Giving love unconditionally means loving your child when he's an angel and when he's a little devil. It means loving her even when you don't love her behavior.

Unconditional love feels limitless in your heart, but it does have boundaries. They are the boundaries you set to teach your child about safety, kindness, and respect.

How Do I Earn Respect?

Being a parent, not a friend, is the way to earn your child's respect.

Love her. Show her you love her. Love her unconditionally.

Be a parent, too. You are in charge.

It often seems that the world is conspiring against you. We live in a disrespectful culture. Politicians campaign with personal attacks rather than reasoned arguments. The media is saturated with examples of people disrespecting the law, themselves, and each other.

You have one place to turn this around: in your own home.

Be a role model. Be loving, authoritative, consistent, and reasonable. Insist on family values; live by them yourself.

Learning to respect you also helps your children to learn to respect themselves. It shows them what respect means. And ultimately, having self-respect will arm your children against the temptations they will meet with their peers and in the wider world.

When your children respect you, they will listen to you. They will learn from you.

Respect goes hand in hand with responsibility. You will be able to prepare them for a happy, satisfying life.

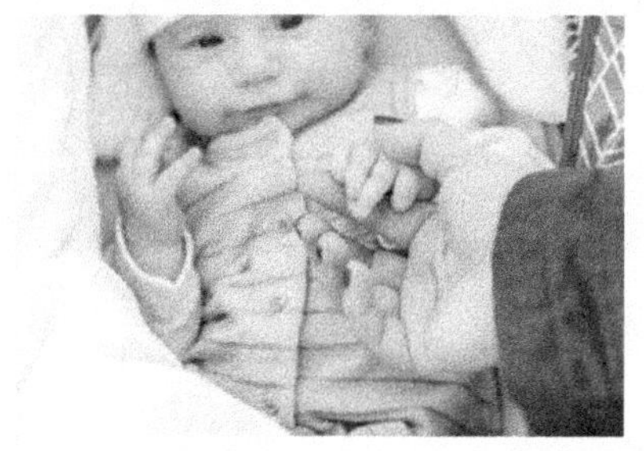

EPILOGUE

THERE'S a powerful story that I heard on National Public Radio's *Story Corps* that sums up for me the essence of being a parent. April Gibson, a single mom, is talking with her 16-year-old son, Gregory Bass (2018)

The story starts with Gregory saying, "We can talk about things for hours. I think I learn more from those conversations than school."

And then he asks his mom, "What did you feel like when I was born?" To which she replies, "When you were born? Um… I actually didn't feel anything."

April was 16 herself when Gregory was born. She had internalized what the world was telling her, that she was bad for being a teenage mom. And so, she tried not to feel anything.

But she goes on to say, "…I just took care of you. I did what I was supposed to do. Until one day I realized that I couldn't believe what people told me about myself ... This is my baby and I love him, and I can feel something. It's not a fairy tale. It's not a failure. It's just a process. And now we're here, 16 years later."

You can hear the emotion in April's voice.

And then, at the end of the story, Gregory says, "When I was little, I was always looking for someone to look up to. But it's always been right in front of me. You're just the greatest person that I ever know. And I just want to be like you." (*Story Corps* website)

What better can a parent hear?

What does it take to be a good parent? It's individual, and it's all the same.

Every child is different. Your child is the only one who can guide you to become the best parent you can be.

As a parent, you do your best to understand and meet that child's needs. But at the end of the day, certain rules guide you along the way:

- Give unconditional love.
- Help them be comfortable with being themselves.
- Back up your love with loving discipline.
- Provide the security of routine.
- Be involved in your children's lives, but don't be intrusive.
- Praise them when they do well.
- Nurture their independence.
- Help your children be involved in the community.
- Make education a priority.
- Never go to sleep upset.
- Always remember, you are the parent.

Your presence is the most important thing you have to give to your children.

When you invest in your children, you're setting them for a balanced adulthood. Your time and your interest, your example, matter far more than material things.

It's like that Harry Chapin song, Cat's in the Cradle: "I'm gonna be like you, dad. You know I'm gonna be like you."

We all start this parenting journey as rank novices. We love them. We do some things right. We make mistakes. We learn as we go.

As your children grow to be more confident, happier, and successful, so do you as a parent.

I have been lucky enough to journey this road twice. A lot has changed in the decade since my first two children grew up and launched into lives of their own. I am proud of them. Now that they are grown, I am proud to be their friend.

Now I'm parenting another child. He's young and has a way to go. But we're getting there and he's doing well.

The other day my son and I were driving back from school. We talk a lot in the car, and the week before I had noticed that my son was coming home mad and acting mean. He got upset about doing his regular chores, and he'd lash out at me and his mom.

Now I knew my son was not a mean person, so I had asked him, "What's wrong?"

He told me that he has a classmate who is a bully, and the bully had started picking on him. Let's call the bully Joe.

"What's happening?" I asked.

He told me that Joe was calling him names and laughing at him for not being good at soccer.

As you can imagine, my first instinct was to pick up the phone, call the principal, and get her to intervene. But then I thought, *no, I can't do that.* My son is going to encounter bullies all his life. If I step in, I may take care of the immediate problem; but that's just showing my son I don't think he can handle it. This kind of thing will happen again. My son needs to know how to stand up to a bully.

So, I sympathized with my son. I told him I knew how awful this made him feel. We talked about different come-backs he might use (and actually had a little fun role-playing). And then I told him a story about my cousin.

My cousin was born with a large birthmark on his jaw. The pediatrician said it could be reduced, but that it would be best to wait until my cousin was at least 12 before doing anything.

One day at school, a bully was taunting my cousin about his birthmark, and my cousin said back to him, "Yeah but you might have one on your butt." That shut the bully up.

I knew when I talked with my son that I may never hear anything about the bullying again. But a week later, while we were driving, he told me proudly, "I told Joe that he might be better at soccer than me, but I was better than him at baseball. And you know, Dad, Joe isn't bothering me anymore."

That's what parenting is all about.

We can't protect our kids from all the trouble in the world. What we can do is prepare them to deal with it.

I take comfort in knowing that, while the world is changing, the fundamental rules of parenting are the same.

Parenting is a journey you take with your child. Every day you get up and start out again.

If you make a mistake, if you raised your voice when you meant to stay calm or snapped out when your child didn't do something right away—it happens. Do better next time.

Let your child see that if you make a mistake, you apologize for your behavior, just as you want them to do.

All we can do is do the best we can.

REFERENCES

All images have been sourced from pexels.com

9 benefits of yoga. (n.d.). Johns Hopkins Medicine. https://www.hopkinsmedicine.org/health/wellness-and-prevention/9-benefits-of-yoga

A look into the science of well-being and the Healthy Minds Framework. (n.d.) Center for Healthy Minds at UW–Madison - Center for Healthy Minds. https://centerhealthyminds.org/about/why-well-being

Achwal, A. (2019, March 26). *8 ways to help your children develop a positive attitude towards life.* First Cry Parenting. https://parenting.firstcry.com/articles/developing-positive-thinking-and-attitude-in-kids-importance-and-tips/

Acupuncture. (2021). John Hopkins Medicine. https://www.hopkinsmedicine.org/health/wellness-and-prevention/acupuncture

Adoption awareness: Handling awkward adoption questions and comments. (2014, September 10). Tapestry Books. https://tapestrybooks.com/adoption-awareness-handling-awkward-adoption-questions-comments/

Andrews, M. A. W. (2010). *Ask the brains.* Scientific American Mind, 21(5), 70–70. https://doi.org/10.1038/scientificamericanmind1110-70

Anware, L. (2018, January 19) *A mother on the challenges of becoming a teenage parent.* Storycorps.org. https://storycorps.org/stories/a-mother-on-the-challenges-of-becoming-a-teenage-parent/

Arlinghaus, K. R., & Johnston, C. A. (2018). *The importance of creating habits and routine.* American Journal of Lifestyle Medicine, 13(2), 142–144. https://doi.org/10.1177/1559827618818044

Baby boomers born from 1957 to 1964 held an average of 12.4 jobs from ages 18 to 54. The Economics Daily: U.S. Bureau of Labor Statistics. (2021, September 3). Www.bls.gov. https://www.bls.gov/opub/ted/2021/baby-boomers-born-from-1957-to-1964-held-an-average-of-12-4-jobs-from-ages-18-to-54.htm

Baumgardner, J. (2017, October 3). *How to avoid raising an entitled child.* First Things First. https://firstthings.org/how-to-avoid-raising-an-entitled-child/

Bindreiff, D. (2018, August 9). *Giving students the keys to control their own learning outcomes.* Houghton Mifflin Harcourt. https://www.hmhco.com/blog/do-students-have-control-over-the-outcome

Blumberg, N. (2021). *Lili Elbe Danish painter.* Britannica. https://www.britannica.com/biography/Lili-Elbe

Bocknek, E. (2020, April 1). *The importance of routines for kids.* Zero to Thrive. https://zerotothrive.org/routines-for-kids/

Branum, A. M., & Lukacs, S. L. (2020). *Products* - Data Briefs - Number 10 - October 2008. Centers for Disease Control and Prevention National Center for Health Statistics. https://www.cdc.gov/nchs/products/databriefs/db10.htm

Brazelton, T. B., & Sparrow, J. (2015). *Discipline: The Brazelton Way.* Lifelong Books, Decapo Press, A Member Of The Perseus Books Group.

Brockell, G. (2019, December 18). *"A republic, if you can keep it": Did Ben Franklin really say Impeachment Day's favorite quote?.* Washington Post. https://www.washingtonpost.com/history/2019/12/18/republic-if-you-can-keep-it-did-ben-franklin-really-say-impeachment-days-favorite-quote/

Brody, J. E. (2016, June 13). *Being transgender as a fact of nature.* Well. https://well.blogs.nytimes.com/2016/06/13/transsexualism-as-a-fact-of-nature/

Brown, C., Goodman, S., & Küpper, L. (2020, March). *The unplanned journey*. Center for Parent Information and Resources. https://www.-parentcenterhub.org/journey/

Brown, M. (2021). *Dad's toddler meltdown reminds parents why you should never go to bed angry*. Parents. https://www.parents.-com/news/dads-toddler-meltdown-reminds-parents-why-you-should-never-go-to-bed-angry/

Chamberlin, J. (2013, September). *"Tiger parenting" doesn't create child prodigies, finds new research*. American Psychological Association. https://www.apa.org/monitor/2013/09/tiger-parenting

Chen, G. (2020, October 5). *10 ways to protect your kids from bullying at school*. Public School Review. https://www.publicschoolreview.-com/blog/10-ways-to-protect-your-kids-from-bullying-at-school

Cheng, A. (2020, September 25). *How to talk so kids will listen book summary, by Adele Faber, Elaine Mazlish. Allen Cheng*. https://www.al-lencheng.com/how-to-talk-so-kids-will-listen-book-summary-adele-faber-elaine-mazlish/

Clayton, D. (2019). *20 things every parent of kids with special needs should hear*. Abilities.com. https://www.abilities.com/community/par-ents-20things.html

Colino, S., Broadwell, L., Schuman, C., & Peck, S. (2015, June 11). *How to deal with bullies: A guide for parents*. Parents. https://www.par-ents.com/kids/problems/bullying/bully-proof-your-child-how-to-deal-with-bullies/

Community service: A family's guide to getting involved. (n.d.). Nemours Kidshealth.org. https://kidshealth.org/en/parents/volun-teer.html

Connect with your community. (2013, May 14). National Geographic Society. https://www.nationalgeographic.org/idea/connect-your-community/

Decades of scientific research that started a growth mindset revolution. (2017). Mindset Works. https://www.mindsetworks.com/science/

Dewar, G. (2019a, November 2). *Homework for young children: Is it justified?* Parenting Science. https://parentingscience.com/homework-for-young-children/

Dewar, G. (2019b, December 2). *The effects of praise: 7 evidence-based tips for using praise wisely.* Parenting Science. https://parentingscience.-com/effects-of-praise/

Dewar, G. (2020, August 22). *Teaching empathy: Evidence-based tips for fostering empathic awareness in children.* Parenting Science. https://parentingscience.com/teaching-empathy-tips/

Different parenting styles: Tiger mom vs. helicopter mom. (2012, February 26). Your Teen Magazine. https://yourteenmag.com/family-life/communication/helicopter-parents-vs-tiger-parents

Different types of yoga and their benefits. (2021). Atlantic Spine and Health Clinic. https://www.atlanticspineclinic.com/chiropractic-blog/344/Different+Types+of+Yoga+and+Their+Benefits

Dimovski, A. (2020, March 21). *19+ eye-opening statistics about career changes in 2021.* Go Remotely. https://goremotely.net/blog/career-change-statistics/

Doer, G. (2019, April 2). *Teaching self-control: Evidence-based tips.* Parenting Science. https://parentingscience.com/teaching-self-control/

Edelman, M. W. (2015, August 21). *It's hard to be what you can't see.* Children's Defense Fund. https://www.childrensdefense.org/child-watch-columns/health/2015/its-hard-to-be-what-you-cant-see/

Employment characteristics of families -2018. (2019). U.S. Department of Labor Bureau of Labor Statistics. https://www.bls.gov/news.release/pdf/famee.pdf

Employment trends by generation: How often do people change jobs? (2021, May 19). PeoplePath. https://www.peoplepath.com/employment-trends-by-generation-how-often-do-people-change-jobs/

Eschner, K. (2017, April 10). *The eighteenth-century founder of homeopathy said his treatments were better than bloodletting.* Smithsonian Magazine. https://www.smithsonianmag.com/smart-news/why-did-eighteenth-century-founder-homeopathy-think-his-theory-medicine-worked-180962794/

Extracurricular participation and student engagement. (1995, June). Ed.gov. https://nces.ed.gov/pubs95/web/95741.asp

Families and households. (2019, October 10). The United States Census Bureau. https://www.census.gov/topics/families/families-and-households.html

Food allergies. (2020, June 8). Centers for Disease Control and Prevention.
https://www.cdc.gov/healthyschools/foodallergies/index.htm

Geiger, M. (2017, February 15). *'How to talk so little kids will listen': advice from the author.* Washington Post. https://www.washingtonpost.com/news/parenting/wp/2017/02/15/how-to-talk-so-little-kids-will-listen-a-qa-with-the-author/

Gender dysphoria | Diagnosis & treatment. (n.d.). Boston Children's Hospital. https://www.childrenshospital.org/conditions-and-treatments/conditions/g/gender-dysphoria/diagnosis-and-treatment

Gersch, D. (2019, April 23). *Body image (children and teens).* Familydoctor.org. https://familydoctor.org/building-your-childs-body-image-and-self-esteem/

Get involved in your child's life. (2021). YES Safe Choices; Lourdes, Fred Akshar, NYS Education Department. http://www.yessafechoices.org/parents/tips-and-tools/get-involved-your-child%E2%80%99s-life

Gilboa, D. (2014). *Get the behavior you want... without being the parent you hate!* : Dr. G's guide to effective parenting. Demos Health.

Himelfarb, E. (2021, July 17). *An age-by-age guide to dealing with "I hate you."* Today's Parent. https://www.todaysparent.com/family/parenting/an-age-by-age-guide-to-dealing-with-i-hate-you/

Hoghughi, M. (1998). *The importance of parenting in child health.* BMJ, 316(7144), 1545–1550. https://doi.org/10.1136/bmj.316.7144.1545

How our parenting has changed over the years. (2020, July 2). Growing Leaders. https://growingleaders.com/blog/how-our-parenting-has-changed-over-the-years/

Improve your child's active listening skills. (2017, July 27). Oxford Learning. https://www.oxfordlearning.com/improve-active-listening-skills/

Jahnke, R., Larkey, L., Rogers, C., Etnier, J., & Lin, F. (2010). A comprehensive review of health benefits of qigong and tai chi. *American Journal of Health Promotion,* 24(6), e1–e25. https://doi.org/10.4278/ajhp.081013-lit-248

Katie. (2018, May 28). *Colors and shapes.* Gift of Curiosity.

https://www.giftofcuriosity.com/why-learning-colors-and-shapes-is-so-important-for-young-children/

Langer, E. (2018, March 13). *T. Berry Brazelton, pediatrician who soothed generations of parents, dies at 99.* Washington Post. https://www.washingtonpost.com/local/obituaries/t-berry-brazelton-pediatrician-who-soothed-generations-of-parents-dies-at-99/2018/03/13/313aa79e-2715-11e8-bc72-077aa4dab9ef_story.html

Lee, T. Y., & Lok, D. P. P. (2012, May 2). Bonding as a positive youth development construct: a conceptual review. *The Scientific World Journal.* https://www.hindawi.com/journals/tswj/2012/481471/

Lehman, J. (n.d.). *"Because I said so." Is this parenting phrase effective?* Empowering Parents. https://www.empoweringparents.com/article/is-this-parenting-phrase-effective-because-i-said-so/

Levine, M. (2020). *Ready or not: preparing our kids to thrive in an uncertain and rapidly changing world.* Harper, An Imprint Of Harpercollins Publishers.

Lott, L., & Intner, R. (2005). *Chores without wars: Turning housework into teamwork.* Taylor Trade Pub.

Meredith, J. (2021, March 22). *4 ways parents put their identity on their kids' shoulders.* USA Football. https://blogs.usafootball.com/blog/8240/4-ways-parents-put-their-identity-on-their-kids-shoulders

Miller, C. (n.d.). *How to help children calm down.* Child Mind Institute. https://childmind.org/article/how-to-help-children-calm-down/

Moore, J. T. (2018). *The power of presence: Be a voice in your child's ear even when you're not with them.* Grand Central Life & Style.

Morin, A. (2021, January 21). *How parents can stop overparenting their kids.* Verywell Family. https://www.verywellfamily.com/signs-that-you-overparenting-your-child-1095052

Moule, J. (2009). *Understanding unconscious bias and unintentional racism.* Phi Delta Kappan, 90(5), 320–326. https://doi.org/10.1177/003172170909000504

Ni, P. (2016, February 28). *10 signs of a narcissistic parent.* Psychology Today. https://www.psychologytoday.com/us/blog/communication-success/201602/10-signs-narcissistic-parent

Number of jobs held, labor market activity, and earnings growth among the youngest baby boomers: Results from a longitudinal survey. (2021). Bureau of Labor Statistics U.S. Department of Labor. https://www.bls.gov/news.release/pdf/nlsoy.pdf

Orson, K. (n.d.). *10 reasons your toddler's tantrum is actually a good thing*. Parents. https://www.parents.com/toddlers-preschoolers/discipline/tantrum/10-reasons-your-toddlers-tantrum-is-actually-a-good-thing/

Parenting in America. (2015, December 17). Pew Research Center's Social & Demographic Trends Project. https://www.pewresearch.org/social-trends/2015/12/17/parenting-in-america/

Pearson, C. (2021, March 29). *4 things parents do that inadvertently raise entitled kids.* HuffPost. https://www.huffpost.com/entry/4-things-parents-do-that-inadvertently-raise-entitled-kids_l_606208a1c5b67593e05b000b

Pennell, J. (2017, November 23). *This is how much Monica's apartment in "Friends" would really cost.* Today.com. https://www.today.com/home/how-much-monica-s-apartment-friends-would-really-cost-t91476

Pierson, E., Simoiu, C., Overgoor, J., Corbett-Davies, S., Jenson, D., Shoemaker, A., Ramachandran, V., Barghouty, P., Phillips, C., Shroff, R., & Goel, S. (2020). A large-scale analysis of racial disparities in police stops across the United States. *Nature Human Behaviour*, 4, 1–10. https://doi.org/10.1038/s41562-020-0858-1

Pincus, D. (n.d.). *How to control your anger with kids.* Empowering Parents. https://www.empoweringparents.com/article/calm-parenting-get-control-child-making-angry/

Policing women: Race and gender disparities in police stops, searches, and use of force. (2019, May 14). Prison Policy Initiative. https://www.prisonpolicy.org/blog/2019/05/14/policingwomen/

Popomaronis, T. (2019, April 5). *Want to raise successful kids? Harvard, MIT study says doing one thing at age 4 could make them happier and wealthier in life.* CNBC. https://www.cnbc.com/2019/04/05/harvard-mit-study-says-parents-do-this-one-thing-to-raise-happier-successful-wealthier-children.html

Reidbord, S. (2016, May 8). *Choose your actions, not your feelings.*

Psychology Today. https://www.psychologytoday.com/us/blog/sacramento-street-psychiatry/201605/choose-your-actions-not-your-feelings

Salleh, M. R. (2008). Life event, stress and illness. *The Malaysian Journal of Medical Sciences: MJMS,* 15(4), 9–18. https://www.ncbi.nlm.nih.gov/pmc/articles/PMC3341916/

Saltsman, T. (2019, October 2). *Why having too many choices is making us miserable.* Fast Company. https://www.fastcompany.com/90411925/having-too-many-choices-is-making-us-miserable

Sierksma, J., Thijs, J., & Verkuyten, M. (2014). Children's intergroup helping: The role of empathy and peer group norms. *Journal of Experimental Child Psychology,* 126, 369–383. https://doi.org/10.1016/j.jecp.2014.06.002

Spock, B. (1946). *The common sense book of baby and child care.* Duell, Sloan And Pearce.

Taylor, J. (2010). *Parenting: Respect starts at home.* Psychology Today. https://www.psychologytoday.com/us/blog/the-power-prime/201001/parenting-respect-starts-home

Test yourself for hidden bias. (2009, September 10). Learning for Justice. https://www.learningforjustice.org/professional-development/test-yourself-for-hidden-bias

The armless archer. (2021, August 22). Www.youtube.com; ViacomCBS. https://www.youtube.com/watch?v=UiT0cKHpeF4

The importance of routine for children. (2017, December 7). KLA Schools. https://www.klaschools.com/importance-of-routine-for-children/

The state of LD: Understanding the 1 in 5. (2017, May 2). NCLD. https://www.ncld.org/news/newsroom/the-state-of-ld-understanding-the-1-in-5

Toole, B. (2019). *Risky play for children: Why we should let kids go outside and then get out of the way.* Canadian Broadcasting Corporation. https://www.cbc.ca/natureofthings/features/risky-play-for-children-why-we-should-let-kids-go-outside-and-then-get-out

Toxic stress. (n.d.). Center on the Developing Child at Harvard University. https://developingchild.harvard.edu/science/key-concepts/toxic-stress/

Truong, D. (2019, July 16). *More students are being bullied online, federal report says.* The Washington Post. https://www.washingtonpost.com/local/education/more-students-are-being-bullied-online-federal-report-says/2019/07/15/0f19f7d0-a71d-11e9-9214-246e594de5d5_story.html

Underwood, P. L. (2020, August 13). *Are you overpraising your child?* The New York Times. https://www.nytimes.com/2020/08/13/parenting/praising-children.html

van Schie, C. C., Jarman, H. L., Huxley, E., & Grenyer, B. F. S. (2020). Narcissistic traits in young people: understanding the role of parenting and maltreatment. *Borderline Personality Disorder and Emotion Dysregulation*, 7(1). https://doi.org/10.1186/s40479-020-00125-7

Voss, P., Thomas, M. E., Cisneros-Franco, J. M., & de Villers-Sidani, É. (2017). Dynamic brains and the changing rules of neuroplasticity: implications for learning and recovery. *Frontiers in Psychology*, 8. https://doi.org/10.3389/fpsyg.2017.01657

Wallace, J. B. (2021, September 17). *Instagram is even worse than we thought for kids. What do we do about it?* Washington Post. https://www.washingtonpost.com/lifestyle/2021/09/17/instagram-teens-parent-advice/

Wei, M. (2016, January 29). *More than just a game: Yoga for school-age children.* Harvard Health Blog. https://www.health.harvard.edu/blog/more-than-just-a-game-yoga-for-school-age-children-201601299055

What the longest study on happiness ever reveals. (2019, September 15). Ignitia Office. https://www.ignitiaoffice.com/what-the-longest-study-on-happiness-reveals/

Why telling family stories to our kids is so important. (2017, May 15). HuffPost UK. https://www.huffingtonpost.co.uk/entry/why-telling-family-stories-to-our-kids-is-so-important_uk_59131710e4b050bdca612fd7

Wikipedia Contributors. (2018, November 30). *Christine Jorgensen.* Wikimedia Foundation. https://en.wikipedia.org/wiki/Christine_Jorgensen

Willard, N., & Harris, N. (2010, November 21). *What is cyberbullying? Everything parents need to know about bullying online.* Parents.

https://www.parents.com/kids/problems/bullying/cyberbullying-101-what-is-cyberbullying/

Williams, W. (2018, May 7). *How are the children?* Www.youtube.-com. https://www.youtube.com/watch?v=dg_tlwk0Uww

Winston, R., & Chicot, R. (2016). The importance of early bonding on the long-term mental health and resilience of children. *London Journal of Primary Care,* 8(1), 12–14. https://doi.org/10.1080/17571472.2015.1133012

Bauer, B. A. (2020, December 15). *Reflexology for stress relief.* Mayo Clinic. https://www.mayoclinic.org/healthy-lifestyle/consumer-health/expert-answers/what-is-reflexology/faq-20058139

Ehmke, R. (2016, February 26). *Tips for beating test anxiety.* Child Mind Institute. https://childmind.org/article/tips-for-beating-test-anxiety/

LeCunff, A.-L. (2019, August 1). *The difference between habits, routines and rituals.* Ness Labs. https://nesslabs.com/habits-routines-rituals

Swanson, R. (2019, October 7). *Perspective | I've opted out of homework for my young children. Here's why, and how you can, too.* Washington Post. https://www.washingtonpost.com/lifestyle/2019/10/07/ive-opted-out-homework-my-young-children-heres-why-how-you-can-too/

ABOUT THE AUTHOR

James Dudelson is a well-known producer and distributor in the TV & Film Industries. He's also a very funny guy, which got him invited to star in his own radio show, *Hollywood Uncut* (at CBS), which was a success. James loved the experience and has mulled over the idea of doing a podcast and write books for several years but could never find the time nor the inspiration… until his son Aaron was born. He launched his *Dad at 65* website and podcast in Spring 2021. This platform is allowing him to explore his humorous views while sharing his multigenerational experience in how to raise children.

Email James (james@dadat65.com) for more info.

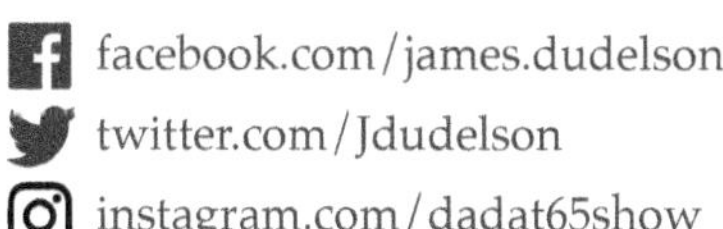

ALSO BY JAMES DUDELSON

Dad at 65 - A Parenting Platform and Podcast

Created by James Dudelson, *Dad At 65* offers parenting tips, personal stories, and current topics all served with a generous dollop of humor.

Visit the website www.DadAt65.com or watch the podcast episodes www.DadAt65.com/podcast.

How to Stop Hating Being a Parent - Free Ebook

In this short and extremely funny mini-guide James Dudelson explores the little discussed issue of parenting dissatisfaction, and shares six tips on how to put back the happy into being a parent.

Free download here: https://www.dadat65.com/blog/how-to-stop-hating-being-a-parent

www.ingramcontent.com/pod-product-compliance
Lightning Source LLC
LaVergne TN
LVHW020643100826
845148LV00012B/2320
9780578354460